THE TOTAL BRAIN WORKOUT

THE
TOTAL
BRAIN
WORKOUT

450 Puzzles to
Sharpen Your Mind,
Improve Your Memory and
Keep Your Brain Fit

by Marcel Danesi, Ph.D.

HARLEQUIN®

HARLEQUIN®

THE TOTAL BRAIN WORKOUT

ISBN-13: 978-0-373-89206-8
ISBN-10: 0-373-89206-3

www.eHarlequin.com

Designed and typeset by Liney Li

Printed in U.S.A.

Contents

Introduction

CROSSWORDS, SUDOKU, ANAGRAMS, BRAINTEASERS, TRIVIA CHALLENGES—the list goes on! These terms are known to virtually everyone. But what you may not know is that such apparently "trivial amusements" also foster brain growth by stimulating logical and creative thinking regions of the brain. Research has, in fact, come forward recently to suggest (although not prove beyond a shadow of a doubt) that puzzles sharpen the mind, improve memory and keep the brain fit throughout life, especially in later life.

As a boomer myself reaching the so-called twilight years, and a puzzle addict since my childhood, I welcome this news. If puzzles are to the brain what physical exercise is to the body, then let's do puzzles—not just for fun, but, more importantly, for brain fitness.

As a professor of anthropology at the University of Toronto, I became fascinated by the ancientness of puzzles and their constant use in cultures throughout the world as tests of intelligence and creative imagination. As a result, I conducted research on puzzles and wrote a number of scholarly books on the topic, finding out in the process how truly ingenious and productive the "puzzle instinct" is in human life. I now teach a course on puzzles at the university, studying every aspect of this instinct and, incidentally, having a lot of fun as I do so. I have also had the opportunity to work with neuroscientists and psychologists over several decades to design puzzle-based teaching and learning methods to help people learn better in various disciplines.

This book is a product of my background experiences with both puzzles and pedagogy. I have constructed the 450 puzzles in it to "stimulate" specific areas of the brain and thus to help you exercise your brain in a methodical fashion. I really believe that this will help keep your brain fit. It is "chicken soup" for your brain.

Each chapter contains puzzle genres that target specific brain areas. For example, visual thinking puzzles (Chapter 2) are designed to set off visual thinking processes that seemingly affect our capacity to learn and remember over time.

There is, of course, no empirical way to demonstrate that a specific puzzle is capable of activating a certain part of the brain for all individuals—unless I were to put your brain through a PET scan as you solve it! Nevertheless, it is my opinion that nothing but beneficial consequences can come out of solving puzzles organized systematically according to brain functions.

WHY PUZZLES?

Since the dawn of civilization, we human beings have been fascinated by puzzles of all kinds. Puzzles from Babylonia (1800–1600 BCE), Egypt (1700–1650 BCE) and the ancient civilizations of the Orient and the Americas have been discovered and shown to be remarkably similar in design. One of the oldest puzzles known to the Western world is the Riddle of the Sphinx. In Greek mythology, the Sphinx was a monster with the head and breasts of a woman, the body of a lion and the wings of a bird. Lying on a rock, she accosted all who were about to enter the city of Thebes by asking them a riddle:

What is it that has four feet at dawn, two at midday, and three at twilight?

Those who failed to answer the riddle correctly were killed on the spot. On the other hand, if anyone were able to come up with the correct answer, the Sphinx vowed to destroy itself. The hero Oedipus solved the riddle by answering, "A human being, who crawls on four limbs as a baby [at the dawn of life], walks upright on two as an adult [at the midday of life] and walks with the aid of a stick in old age [at the twilight of life]," and the Sphinx killed itself. For ridding them of this terrible monster, the Thebans made Oedipus their king.

Throughout history, puzzles have captivated the fancy of many famous personages: Charlemagne, the founder of the Holy Roman Empire; Edgar Allan Poe, the great American writer; Lewis Carroll, who is best known for his two great children's books, *Alice's Adventures in Wonderland* and *Through the Looking Glass;* and Benjamin Franklin, the American statesman, entrepreneur and publisher, among many others. This fascination with puzzles continues today, as witnessed by the widespread popularity of puzzle magazines, brain-challenging sections in newspapers, puzzle books for children and adults alike, TV quiz shows, game tournaments and so on. Millions of people the world over simply seem to enjoy solving puzzles for their own sake. As the great British puzzlist Henry E. Dudeney (1857–1930) aptly put it, "A good puzzle, like virtue, is its own reward."

PUZZLES AND THE BRAIN

The brain is a marvelous organ, but, like all organs, it needs to stay in shape, so to speak. In recent years many scientists have documented studies showing that doing puzzles enhances brain activity. I have undertaken "anecdotal experiments" by suggesting puzzle solving as a way to enhance or improve mental functions. One example hits very close to home; I suggested to a relative suffering from a debilitating brain-degenerative disease that he do crosswords. Before passing away, he became fascinated with doing them (for the first time in his life, by the way), and I was told by his wife that puzzle solving not only seemed to slow down the brain degeneration from which he was suffering but also enriched his life, giving him something interesting to do. Although such incidences in no way constitute "scientific" evidence about the power of puzzles to enhance brain functions, they fit in with the pattern of results that more technical research studies are documenting.

The puzzles in this book are organized to give you a steady and graduated workout that is consistent with what the scientific research on brain functioning says. Like a physical workout, each chapter allows you to start off nice and easy, getting you to work up to the more complex levels gradually. These nine "sessions of brainteasing exercises," as they can be called, will boost reasoning skills, memory and mental processing speed. This is backed up by numerous studies, including one conducted by Michael Marsiske at the University of Florida at Gainesville and Sherry Willis at Pennsylvania State University that was published in the *Journal of the American Medical Association* in 2006. The study showed that doing puzzle-type exercises, graduated in a consistent fashion as in this book, staved off mental decline, bolstered the brain and sharpened logical skills in adults over fifty in the same way that physical exercise protects and strengthens the aging body. The study also suggested that benefits accrued to the pre-fifty population as well.

To reap the benefits, the study suggested, people need to progress from easy puzzle exercises to harder ones, which is just what we have done in this book. The book has, in other words, a "hidden structure" that allows you, chapter by chapter, to build brain power in ways that are consistent with the above-mentioned study and many others like it. So, let this book do its work on you by starting from the very first easy word-search puzzles to very complex logic and math brainteasers.

If you want more brain-based puzzles and games after you have worked through this book—consider it a basic training manual in puzzle solving—you can get more by visiting these two Web sites: www.sharpbrains.com and www.happy-neuron.com.

HOW TO USE THIS BOOK

In all, there are 450 puzzles for you to solve in this book. They are organized into nine chapters, each containing fifty puzzles that have a specific brain-based objective built into them. The fifty puzzles in Chapter 1 are designed to help activate the language areas of the brain, for example, whereas those in Chapter 2 are designed to stimulate visual thinking areas. Chapters 3, 4, 5 and 6 involve logical thinking of various kinds. Chapter 6 contains one of the most popular of all contemporary puzzle genres—Sudoku. Chapter 7 presents your mathematical brain with classic conundrums to solve, while Chapters 8 and 9 involve linguistic and cultural knowledge. The book ends with an answer key, so you can check your responses to all of the puzzles.

Each chapter starts off with a brief summary of what is known about a certain function or faculty (such as language or perception) and what features of the puzzles fit with the related research. This is followed by five puzzle sections, usually organized in order of difficulty (unless puzzles of a certain genre cannot be organized in this way). The reason for this is obvious: as you become familiar with the structure of a genre through easy puzzles, you can then use this knowledge to really put your brain to work!

Facility comes with practice, and 450 puzzles organized according to brain functions will certainly give you this. At the same time, they will, I hope, also provide mental recreation. Have fun!

1
VERBAL THINKING

The brain is wider than the sky.
EMILY DICKINSON

THE LEFT HEMISPHERE OF THE BRAIN IS WHERE THE MAJOR LANGUAGE FUNCTIONS are located. The discovery of these functions started in 1861, when the surgeon Pierre Paul Broca identified an area in that hemisphere where speech articulation is located. It is, logically, named after him (Broca's area). In 1874, the German neurologist Carl Wernicke discovered another left-hemispheric area that involved speech comprehension. This too is known after its discoverer (Wernicke's area).

These two areas, along with others, are responsible for how we produce and understand sounds, words and sentences. Both hemispheres are needed in a cooperative way to produce complex thinking, but there is little doubt that, when it comes to controlling many specific language skills (although not all), the left hemisphere is the primary one involved. Research has also shown that the right hemisphere, with its creative abilities, is involved during the initial stages of imaginative language tasks such as those required in puzzle solving. There are plenty of implications for brain fitness.

The fifty puzzles in this chapter are designed to stimulate language areas of the brain. Let's get going!

WORD SEARCHES

You have probably seen a word search. It is a square arrangement of what looks like random letters, but there are words hidden among the letters. They can be read horizontally, from left to right or right to left; vertically, from top to bottom or from the bottom up; and diagonally, in both directions. All you have to do is locate the words.

There are various levels of difficulty involved. The easiest puzzle is the one that gives you the words. A harder type gives you clues related to the hidden words, but not the words themselves. You might find other legitimate words in a puzzle in addition to the required ones. These have been put there simply to confuse you. You do not need to circle them. The puzzles will start off easy and gradually become harder to solve. Good luck!

1. The following ten words (all colors) are hidden in this puzzle. They can be read either from left to right or in a downward direction only, and the words do not cross. The first one is circled for you.

RED	ORANGE
YELLOW	BROWN
BLUE	WHITE
GREEN	BLACK
PURPLE	INDIGO

```
G R E E N S U O P C C U R
W Q R T A T G H U R B P E
A O R A N G E O R O R C D
S L L O D V P H P W O P D
D L U I E A G U L N W P B
Y E L L O W G H E I N P L
G Y I I O E B N T D C C A
H H S O I N D I G O A L C
W A S B L U E C S D C C K
B R T Y U I L U E D V B M
C A D W H I T E S C A D S
```

2. The following ten words (all kinship terms) can be read from left to right, right to left and upward or downward. Again, the words do not cross.

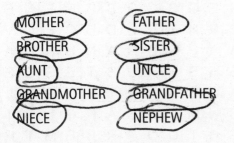

MOTHER   FATHER

BROTHER   SISTER

AUNT   UNCLE

GRANDMOTHER   GRANDFATHER

NIECE   NEPHEW

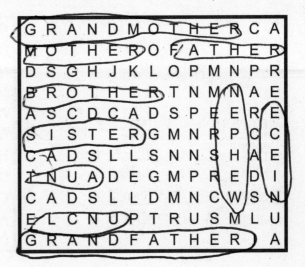

G R A N D M O T H E R C A
M O T H E R O F A T H E R
D S G H J K L O P M N P R
B R O T H E R T N M N A E
A S C D C A D S P E E R E
S I S T E R G M N R P C C
C A D S L L S N N S H A E
I N U A D E G M P R E D I
C A D S L L D M N C W S N
E L C N U P T R U S M L U
G R A N D F A T H E R A

3. The following ten words (all names of academic subjects) can be read from left to right, right to left, upward or downward and diagonally in any direction. Again, the words do not cross.

HISTORY   LITERATURE

CHEMISTRY   PHYSICS

GEOGRAPHY   ARITHMETIC

GEOMETRY   LANGUAGE

BIOLOGY   ASTRONOMY

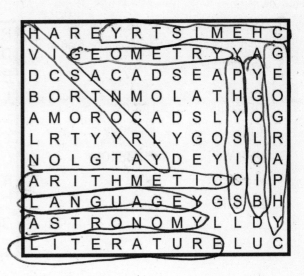

H A R E Y R T S I M E H C
V I G E O M E T R Y Y A G
D C S A C A D S E A P Y E
B O R T N M O L A T H G O
A M O R O C A D S L Y O G
L R T Y Y R L Y G O S L R
N O L G T A Y D E Y I O A
A R I T H M E T I C C I P
L A N G U A G E Y G S B H
A S T R O N O M Y L L D Y
L I T E R A T U R E L U C

4. The following ten words (all having to do with plants or parts of plants) can be read in any direction. This time, the words might cross.

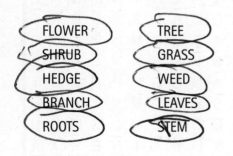

FLOWER   TREE

SHRUB   GRASS

HEDGE   WEED

BRANCH   LEAVES

ROOTS   STEM

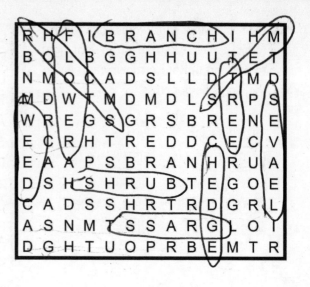

```
R H F I B R A N C H I H M
B O L B G G H H U U T E T
N M O C A D S L L D T M D
M D W T M D M D L S R P S
W R E G S G R S B R E N E
E C R H T R E D D C E C V
E A A P S B R A N H R U A
D S H S H R U B T E G O E
C A D S S H R T R D G R L
A S N M T S S A R G L O I
D G H T U O P R B E M T R
```

5. The following ten words (referring to computers or the Internet) can be read in any direction and can cross.

SOFTWARE   LAPTOP

MOUSE   MEMORY

HARDWARE   CHATROOM

WEBSITE   BLOG

NAVIGATE   GOOGLE

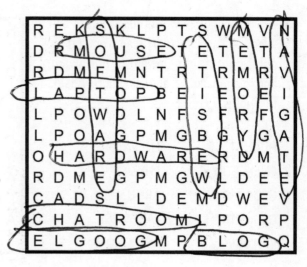

```
R E K S K L P T S W M V N
D R M O U S E T E T E T A
R D M F M N T R T R M R V
L A P T O P B E I E O E I
L P O W D L N F S F R F G
L P O A G P M G B G Y G A
O H A R D W A R E R D M T
R D M E G P M G W L D E E
C A D S L L D E M D W E V
C H A T R O O M L P O R P
E L G O O G M P B L O G Q
```

6. Ten words are hidden in this puzzle, but they are not given below. Instead, the following clues will help you find them. The words can go in any direction and can cross.

CLUES

1. All ten words refer to professions.
2. The longest words have nine letters in them, and there are three of them.
3. The shortest words have six letters in them, and there are five of them.
4. The other two words have eight letters in them.
5. Two words begin with the letter *a* and two with the letter *b*.
6. Alphabetically, the last word starts with *w*.

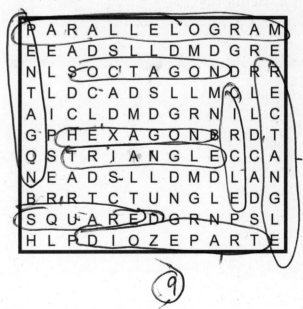

```
A R T I S T U O L B E U R
R W O T A T G H A R N P E
C O S S N G E N L O G C T
H L S O S V K B U W I P I
I E I E E G R U C N P R
T E F T R I F I R I E P W
E Y O I O G B O T P E C A
C H R O G N D E R O R L L
T A P B L E E R O P C O O
L L A W Y E R G U O M N P
A W R S M U S I C I A N G
B N O P A R R O T C O D S
B I O L O G I S T N M S A
```

7. There are ten words hidden in this puzzle, and, again, you have to figure out what they are. The words can go in any direction and can cross.

CLUES

1. All ten words refer to geometrical figures.
2. The longest word has thirteen letters in it. It starts with *p*, as does one other word.
3. Three words end in -*gon*.
4. The two smallest words have six letters in them.
5. Two words, not mentioned in any of the clues above, begin with *t*.
6. The remaining two words have seven and nine letters in them.

```
P A R A L L E L O G R A M
E E A D S L L D M D G R E
N L S O C T A G O N D R R
T L D C A D S L L M O L E
A I C L D M D G R N I L C
G P H E X A G O N B R D T
Q S T R I A N G L E C C A
N E A D S L L D M D L A N
B R R T C T U N G L E D G
S Q U A R E D G R N P S L
H L P D I O Z E P A R T E
```

8. The ten words hidden in this puzzle are all verbs relating to motion. Synonyms or near synonyms for each one and the number of letters in each (shown in parentheses) are provided. The words can go in any direction and can cross.

CLUES

SPRINT (3) ✓

STROLL (4) ✓

WALK BRISKLY (4) ✓

GO ON, GO FORWARD (7) ✓

SCURRY (7) ✓

DASH (6) ✓

GO FAST (5) ✓

LEAP (4) ✓

SLOW DOWN (10) ✓

PICK UP (10) ✓

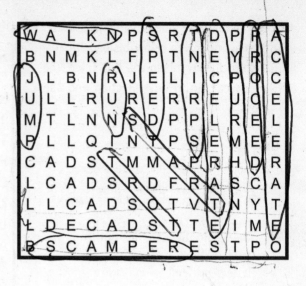

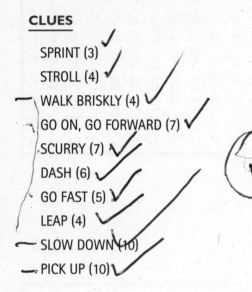

9. The ten words hidden in this puzzle all refer to the media. A clue or definition for each one as well as the number of letters in each (shown in parentheses) is provided. The words can go in any direction and can cross.

CLUES

1. It is put out daily or weekly. (9)
2. It was invented by Marconi. (5)
3. Colloquially, it is called "the box." (10)
4. It is a network linking computer networks. (8)
5. It is another name for a periodical. (8)
6. It can come in hardback or paperback. (4)
7. The only name used for this device before the advent of CDs. (6)
8. It is another name for the movies. (6)
9. It is sometimes called a PC. (8)
10. It is a TV system that transmits to subscribers. (5)

```
A R S C D R C A D S L C L
N E W S P A P E R M D I I
R C D P T D W W I N M N N
N O Q N O I S I V E L E T
W R Y Y P O C A D S L M E
M D N B V C X Z S C D A R
P N Y T S A E O U A L I N
M A G A Z I N E B B N K E
N B V C X Z S T Y L V O T
P N Y T S A E Q U E R O G
C O M P U T E R Q W I B K
```

10. This last word search is a challenging one. The only information provided is that there are ten words in it, referring to kitchen utensils and objects.

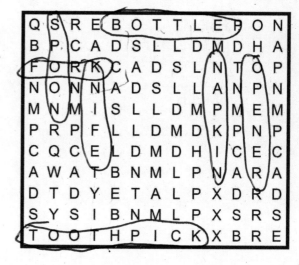

```
Q S R E B O T T L E P O N
B P C A D S L L D M D H A
F O R K C A D S L N T O P
N O N N A D S L L A N P N
M N M I S L L D M P M E M
P R P F L L D M D K P N P
C Q C E L D M D H I C E C
A W A T B N M L P N A R A
D T D Y E T A L P X D R D
S Y S I B N M L P X S R S
T O O T H P I C K X B R E
```

7

A jumbled-word puzzle is, as its name implies, a puzzle in which you have to unscramble a word whose letters have been jumbled to form a real word.

Here's what's involved in this particular version. You are given four jumbles. Unscramble each one, which appears on top of a grid, to form an ordinary word and insert the letters of that word into the cells of its grid. The highlighted letters in the four grids, when joined together, will form the answer to the given question or to the incomplete phrase.

The difficulty level in all of these puzzles is about the same. Some people find these puzzles very easy to solve, while others find them very hard. Word jumbles do, nevertheless, provide a good mental workout for everybody.

11. Studying math can present a lot of _____.

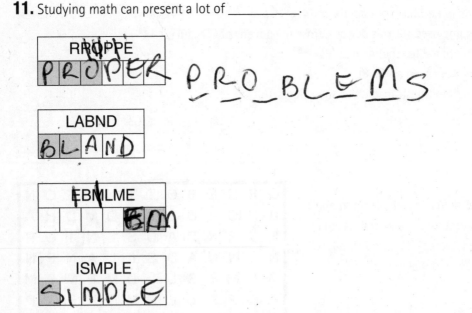

RRØPPE — PROPER — PRO_BLEMS

LABND — BLAND

EBMLME — BM

ISMPLE — SIMPLE

12. What you might get when you do too many puzzles! _____

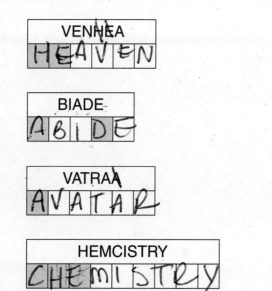

VENHEA
HEAVEN

BIADE
ABIDE

VATRAA
AVATAR

HEMCISTRY
CHEMISTRY

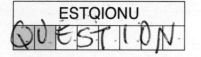

HE A D A CHE

13. The Knights of the Round Table were on a *QUEST* to find the Holy Grail.

ESTQIONU
QUESTION

ATEEST
ESTATE

PLESIM
SIMPLE

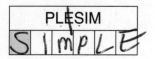

RECTRCO
CORRECT

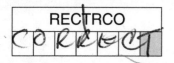

14. Eponymous word, derived from a Dickens character, referring to a personality trait: _____

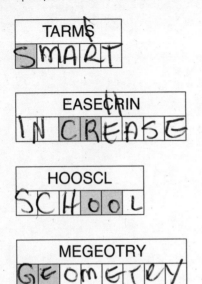

TARMS
SMART

EASECRIN
INCREASE

HOOSCL
SCHOOL

MEGEOTRY
GEOMETRY

SCROOGE

15. The love candy *par excellence:* _____

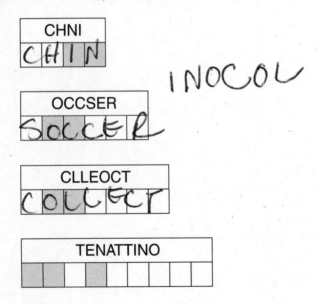

CHNI
CHIN

INOCOL

OCCSER
SOCCER

CLLEOCT
COLLECT

TENATTINO

16. What pop culture buffs of every kind (movie buffs, for example) collect: _____

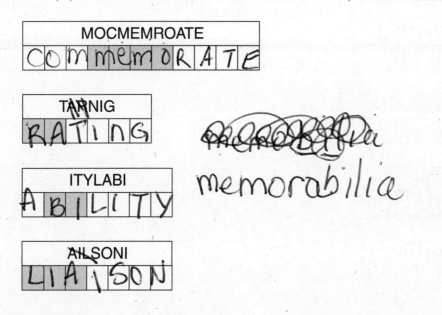

| MOCMEMROATE |
| C O M M E M O R A T E |

| TARNIG |
| R A T I N G |

| ITYLABI |
| A B I L I T Y |

| AILSONI |
| L I A I S O N |

memorabilia

17. An Italian dish: _____

| ECTASP |
| |

| ALLCING |
| |

| PAHPINSSE |
| |

| TIONNINET |
| |

18. "If you don't shape up, it's _____ ," said the boss.

PLECOMTE

MMERSUITME

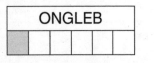
SummeRTime

NAITCON

WERSAN

19. Dance art: _____

ONGLEB

ALCLNIG

ERECSIN

TISINS

20. It's all about coins: _____

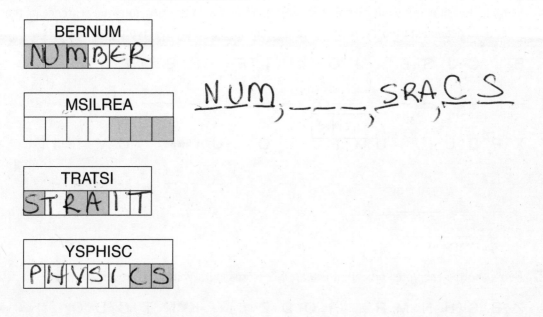

BERNUM
NUMBER

MSILREA

NUM, ___, SRA, CS

TRATSI
STRAIT

YSPHISC
PHYSICS

CRYPTOGRAMS

Cryptograms are secret code puzzles. Secret codes have a long and fascinating history. The sacred Jewish writers, for instance, concealed their messages by using a secret code called *atbash,* in which they would substitute one letter of the Hebrew alphabet for another. For example, they would use the last letter in place of the first, the second last for the second, and so on. Another type of cryptogram is known as a Caesar cipher, because none other than Julius Caesar, the Roman emperor, invented it.

✳ Sample Cryptogram

As an example of a cryptogram, let's figure out what English word the following sequence of letters encodes:

J G N N Q

— — — — —

The word was encoded by replacing each of its letters with the second letter after it in the normal alphabetic sequence. *J* represents *H* (two letters down), *G* represents *E* (two letters down), *N* means *L* (two letters down), and *Q* means *O* (two letters down). Thus, the hidden word is *hello.* ✳

21. This cryptogram conceals an English proverb. There are eleven words in it. If you get stuck, start by trying to figure out what grammatical words are logical in the structure of a sentence (a, the, in, etc.). To get you started, *A* (in the proverb) is encoded as *B* (in the cryptogram).

B   C J S E   J O   U I F   I B O E   J T

_   _ _ _ _   _ _   _ _ _   _ _ _ _   _ _

X P S U I   U X P   J O   U I F   C V T I.

_ _ _ _ _   _ _ _   _ _   _ _ _   _ _ _ _.

22. Here's another encrypted proverb. There are five words in it. What's the proverb?

Z B S H N M R   R O D Z J   K N T C D Q

_ _ _ _ _ _ _   _ _ _ _ _   _ _ _ _ _ _

S G Z M   V N Q C R.

_ _ _ _   _ _ _ _ _.

23. Here's the title of a famous American movie that has been encrypted. There are four words in it. What's the movie?

I Q P G   Y K V J   V J G   Y K P F

_ _ _ _   _ _ _ _   _ _ _   _ _ _ _

24. Here's a famous saying by a French philosopher that has been encrypted. There are five words in it. What's the saying?

M   X L M R O,   X L I V I J S V I   M

_   _ _ _ _ _,   _ _ _ _ _ _ _ _ _   _

E Q.

_ _.

Another type of cryptogram puzzle involves replacing numbers with letters instead of other letters. A specific number will correspond to a specific letter. For example, if you establish that 1 = *H*, then you can go ahead and substitute *H* for each occurrence of the digit 1 in the remaining parts of the cryptogram.

POLYBIUS CIPHER

The number-to-letter cipher is known as a Polybius cipher because it is attributed to the Greek historian Polybius (c. 200–118 BCE).

25. The encoded message conceals the title of a Shakespearean play. There are five words in the title. What's the play? As a clue, *S* = 3.

1 2 2 ' 3   4 5 2 2   6 7 1 6   5 8 9 3

_ _ _ ' _   _ _ _ _   _ _ _ _   _ _ _ _

4 5 2 2

_ _ _ _

26. This message hides a quotation by Irish writer Oscar Wilde. There are twelve words in it. Some of the letters have not been encoded; they have been left in their original spots in the quotation. Use them to help you figure out the code.

2 1 4   1 R T   9 S   1   7 R 5 1 T

_ _ _   _ _ _   _ _   _   _ _ _ _ _

4 5 1 L   W O R S 5   T 8 1 N   N O   1 R T

_ _ _ _   _ _ _ _ _   _ _ _ _   _ _   _ _ _

1 T   1 L L.

_ _   _ _ _.

27. This message conceals an eleven-word quotation by British writer Virginia Woolf. Only the vowels have been encoded. The consonants are not encoded and have been left in their original spots in the quotation.

G R 2 1 T   B 4 D 3 2 S   4 F   P 2 4 P L 2

_ _ _ _   _ _ _ _ _ _   _ _   _ _ _ _ _ _

1 R 2   N 2 V 2 R   R 2 S P 4 N S 3 B L 2

_ _ _   _ _ _ _ _   _ _ _ _ _ _ _ _ _ _

F 4 R   W H 1 T   T H 2 Y   D 4 .

_ _ _   _ _ _ _   _ _ _ _   _ _.

28. Below is an encrypted thirteen-word proverb from ancient India. This time, only the consonants have been encoded; the vowels have not and have been left in their original spots in the quotation. What's the proverb?

1 I 2 E   I 3   A   4 5 I 6 7 E.   8 5 O 3 3

_ _ _ _   _ _   _   _ _ _ _ _ _.   _ _ _ _ _

O 9 E 5   I 10 ,   4 U 10   4 U I 1 6   11 O

_ _ _ _   _ _ ,   _ _ _   _ _ _ _ _   _ _

12 O U 3 E   O 11   I 10 .

_ _ _ _ _   _ _   _ _.

29. This message veils a fifteen-word quotation from American writer Maya Angelou. Some of the letters have not been encoded; they have been left in their original spots in the quotation.

3 6   7 4 5   8 1 9 2   4 N L 7   4 N 2

_ _   _ _ _   _ _ _ _   _ _ _ _   _ _ _

S M 3 L 2   3 N   7 4 5,   G 3 9 2   3 T

_ _ _ _ _   _ _   _ _ _,   _ _ _ _   _ _

T 4   T H 2   P 2 4 P L 2   7 4 5

_ _   _ _ _   _ _ _ _ _ _   _ _ _

L 4 9 2.

_ _ _ _.

30. The next encrypted message veils a seven-word Spanish proverb. Some of the letters have not been encoded; they have been left in their original spots in the quotation.

6 L 1 T T 5 R Y   M 1 K 5 S   6 R 9 5 N 4 S

_ _ _ _ _ _ _   _ _ _ _ _   _ _ _ _ _ _

1 N 4   T R U T H   M 1 K 5 S

_ _ _   _ _ _ _ _   _ _ _ _ _

5 N 5 M 9 5 S.

_ _ _ _ _ _ _.

ODD ONE OUT

In each set of five words, one does not fit in for some reason. The idea is to spot a logical pattern of some kind in the five words. It may be in the structure of the words themselves. For example, four of the words might contain the vowel *U*, while the fifth one does not. Or the pattern may be in the meanings, such as four of the words referring to planets, but not the fifth.

The difficulty level is about the same for all of these puzzles—probably hard if you have never done this kind before. This type of puzzle involves not just verbal thinking, but logical thinking as well.

31. spill, cusp, blame, aspect, inspire

32. scarlet, blue, vermilion, crimson, coral

33. limp, drop, plain, like, true

34. orange, carrot, bean, squash, potato

35. balloon, sphere, globe, cube, marble

36. avid, era, island, try, underneath

37. send, comprehend, catch, impend, trend

38. water, clay, fluid, drink, serum

39. away, easy, aha, data, manna

40. cup, bowl, box, pole, vase

WORD SEQUENCES

These puzzles are variants of the previous ones. This time, you are given four words in a row, each of which is related to the one previous to it in some way. You are given two choices to complete the five-word sequence. The goal is to figure out which of the two comes next in the sequence.

⊛ **Sample Word Sequences**

As in the previous set, the pattern might involve the structure of the words themselves. For example, the four given words might start with the first four vowels in order (**aim**, **ease**, **irk**, **old**). If given the two choices *under* or *over*, you would choose *under*, since it starts with the fifth vowel.

The pattern may also be semantic. For example, if given the sequence *infant, child, teenager, adult,* with the two choices *senior* and *junior,* you would choose *senior.* Why? Because the words in the sequence refer to the stages of life in chronological order—we start off as infants, then become children, and so on. ⊛

41. sun, bun, fun, run, . . .

   (1) pan

   (2) pun

42. arrive, immortal, attire, bass, . . .

    (1) connect

    (2) deem

43. four, nine, leaf, tree, . . .

    (1) nice

    (2) branch

44. I, am, two, call, . . .

    (1) build

    (2) appearance

45. boy, man, mister, gent, . . .

    (1) gal

    (2) guy

46. the, girl, loves, watching, . . .

    (1) movies

    (2) she

47. scientist, Italian, inventor, controversial, . . .

    (1) musician

    (2) Galileo

48. wow, dad, tot, pop, . . .

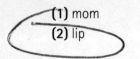

(1) mom

(2) lip

49. answer, bright, crewcut, daring, . . .

(1) afraid

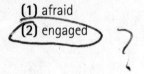

(2) engaged

50. at, par, span, latch, . . .

(1) crabby

(2) creamy

2
VISUAL
THINKING

Nothing exists until or unless it is observed.
WILLIAM BURROUGHS

H OW GOOD ARE YOU AT SPOTTING PATTERNS or anomalies in pictures or images? The ability to do so is controlled mainly by the right hemisphere of the brain—the so-called "visual hemisphere." Various areas in the right hemisphere control how we perceive edges and forms.

Visual thinking is very important for activating such areas and, needless to say, contributes to overall brain functioning. The fifty puzzles in this chapter are designed to bring about some of that activation. In other words, they will help hone your visual logic and problem-solving skills to get your eyes to recognize what is really there in front of you.

OPTICAL ILLUSIONS

An optical illusion is any figure or drawing that dupes the viewer into misinterpreting it in some way. Following are a few classic optical illusions for you to figure out. Their solution, or, more accurately, their proper perception, requires you to interpret mentally what your eyes apparently see.

1. How many figures do you see?

3

2. Are the four lines below perpendicular (upright) or slanting slightly?

3. Which of the two lines below is longer, AB or CD?

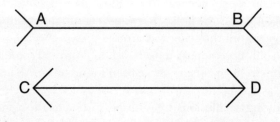

4. Which line, AB or BC, is longer?

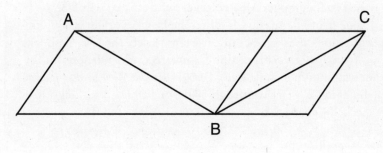

5. Are the two lines above and below the dot in the center of the figure parallel or bulging?

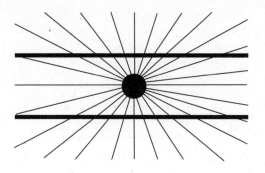

ARE OPTICAL ILLUSIONS CULTURAL?

Today, brain researchers call these illusions *perceptual* rather than *optical*, because it is the brain that intervenes to interpret what the eyes perceive, not the other way around.

Some illusions appear to be based on culture. People living in some non-Western cultures have been found to see AB and CD in puzzle 3 as equal. They are obviously not fooled by the chevrons.

Many optical illusions are probably caused by the technique of *perspective drawing,* which is intended to fool the eye into seeing depth in a two-dimensional drawing.

The figure in puzzle 1 is called an *ambiguous figure.* Scientists call the illusion it produces a figure-ground confusion. Are the facial profiles that you see at certain moments part of the goblet or part of the background? Maybe both. The figure in puzzle 7 is also an ambiguous figure. It is called the Necker Cube, named after the Swiss crystallographer Albert Necker, who created it in 1832.

The figure in puzzle 6 is called the Devil's Fork. It is an example of an *impossible figure,* because it seems to defy the laws of physics.

If you love this sort of thing, some recommendations for further exploration include *Seeing Double: Over 200 Mind-Bending Illusions,* by Richard J. Block (Routledge, 2002), or *Incredible Visual Illusions,* by Al Seckel (Capella, 2007).

6. Put your hand over the left side of the figure below. Then put your hand over the right side. What do you see?

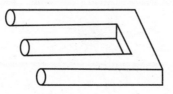

7. What do you see in the figure below? Blink your eyes to see if the image changes.

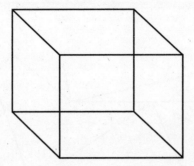

FIGURE DETECTION PUZZLES

In the next set of puzzles, you will be asked to indicate how many figures (or letters) of a certain kind are found in a particular drawing or configuration—how many triangles, how many squares and so on. These puzzles are much harder than you might expect.

8. Count the triangles of any size in the figure below. Hint: Count the triangles from smallest to largest. And don't forget the biggest one of all (a common oversight).

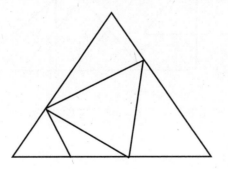

9. Count the number of distinct lines in the figure below.

10. Count the number of triangles.

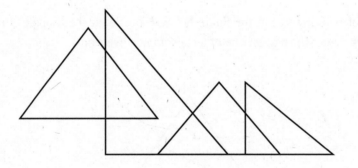

11. Count how many distinct cubes you see in the figure.

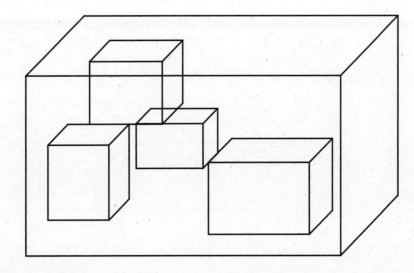

12. This one is a bit harder than the previous ones, even though it may not seem like it. How many triangles do you see?

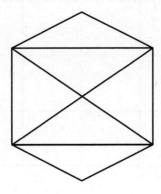

13. This one is harder still. How many triangles do you see this time?

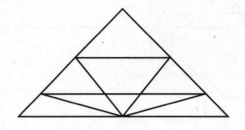

14. How many four-sided 90° figures (squares and rectangles) do you see in the diagram below? Be careful, since there are various sizes of four-sided figures involved.

15. How many four-sided 90° figures (squares and rectangles) do you see in the diagram below?

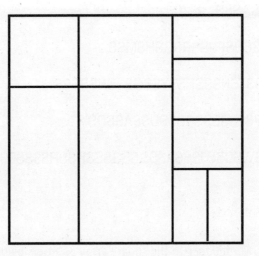

16. How many circles are in the diagram below?

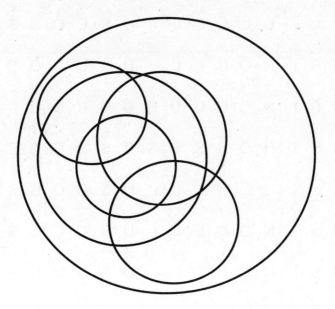

17. Count how many times the letter *S* appears in the mix below.

SSASSS

SSBSSSCSS FSSSRSGSHSMSS

SSESSTSNSSSRSSYSSGSSSNSSSSS

SSSSSASSSSSBSSSCSSDSSASSDS

SSDSGSWSCSSJSSSASSS SSGSSSHSSRSSSSSPSQSSSLSS

18. Find the eight-letter word hidden in the square array of letters below.

I I I I I I L L L L L L I L L S S S U

L L L L I L I I L U U S I N I O S I U

L L L L I L L L L L I U S O O S S S U

L U U S I N O L L L I U S O O O S I U

L U U S I N O U U U U U U U N S S S U

L U U S I N O S S S S S S S O O S I U

I I I I I I L I L L I U S O O S S S U

L U U S I N O O L L I U S O O O S I U

L U U S I N O N L L I U S O O U S O O

I I I I I I L L L L L L I L L S S S U

19. Count the number of eight balls in the mix below.

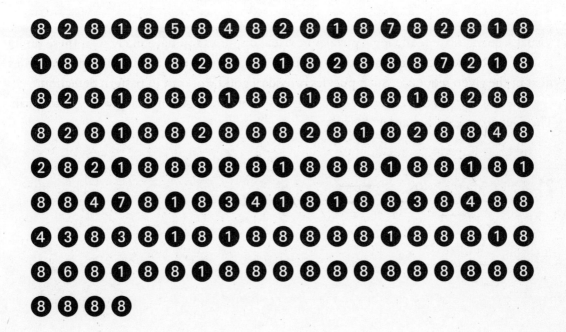

20. For the last puzzle in this category, let's turn up the difficulty level considerably. How many different triangles do you see in the pentagon below? Be careful, as there are many more than meet the eye (pun intended). This one was created by a famous puzzlist named Boris Kordemsky.

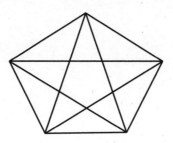

Visual sequences are really logic puzzles in visual disguise. You have likely seen these on IQ tests of various kinds. The goal is to figure out what given figure, (1) or (2), logically comes next in the given sequence. Such puzzles provide a good workout in pattern detection.

The first few puzzles are really easy, to get you into the right mental groove, so to speak. They get progressively harder thereafter.

21.

1.

2.

22.

1.

2.

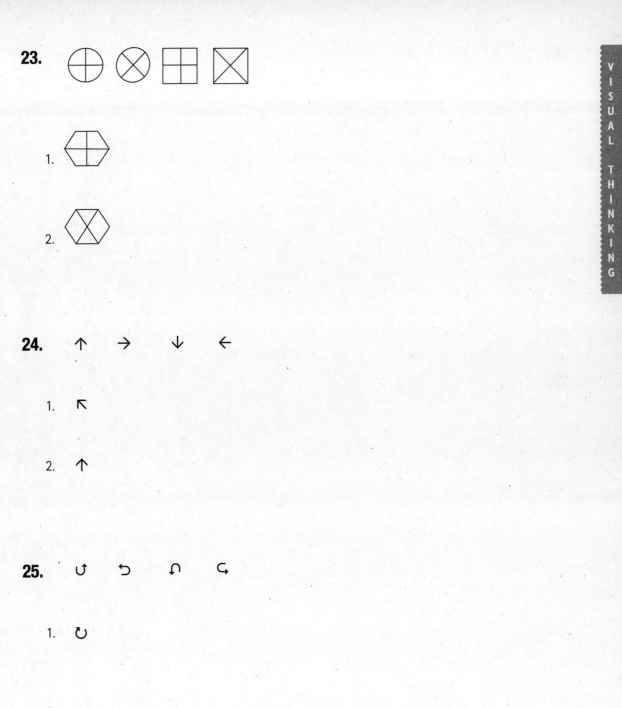

26.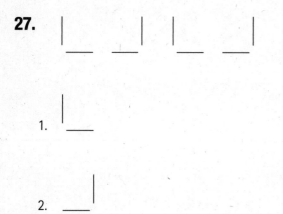

1.

2.

27.

1.

2.

28. ▲△△　▽▼▼　◁◀◁　▲▲△

1.　▶▶▷

2.　▷▷▶

29. ⊃　⊇　⊂　⊆

1.　⨃

2.　∩

30. This is a tricky one.

▭　⬭　◇　◖

1. 　▱

2. 　☾

Puzzles that require removing or modifying the position of certain sticks to create a new figure or something with a new meaning are classics in the visual puzzle category. Here is a set of such puzzles for you to solve. Be careful, as some of them might involve a play on words as well.

31. There are twelve sticks forming the outline of the square figure below. Remove two sticks to make three squares.

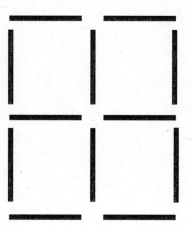

32. There are five sticks below standing upright. Adjust them to make eight.

33. Reposition two sticks in this figure to get two triangles and two squares.

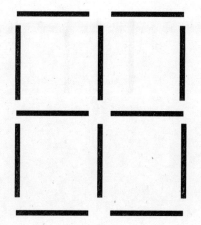

34. How do you get two with these four sticks?

35. How do you get one with these four sticks?

36. How do you get four with these three sticks?

37. Make one-half with these four sticks.

38. Make ten with just two of them.

39. Below is the fraction one-seventh in Roman numerals. Get one from this fraction by repositioning just one stick.

40. The next puzzle is a bit challenging. It was invented by Angelo John Lewis and can be found in his book *Puzzles Old and New* (1893). Fifteen small, thin, wooden rods are laid on a table forming five identical squares. Remove three rods so as to leave only three such squares.

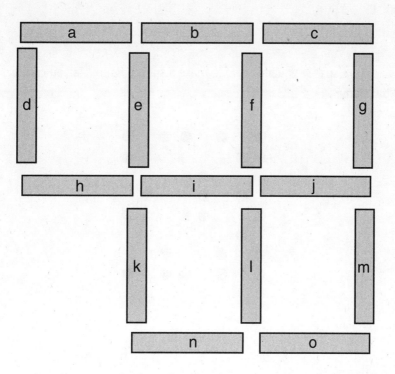

VISUALIZATION PUZZLES

With this last set of puzzles involving mental visualization of some kind, the workout in visual thinking comes to an end. Be careful! Some are tricks.

41. How many balls will you need to add to the triangle to get a rectangle?

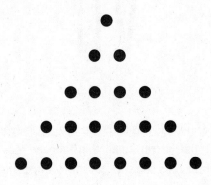

42. The balls below are spaced equally apart to make a square figure. As you can see, some balls are missing. How many?

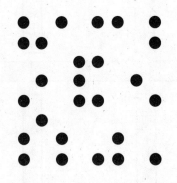

43. There are four overlapping circles below. In how many of them does A occur? In how many does B occur? In how many does C occur? And in how many does D occur?

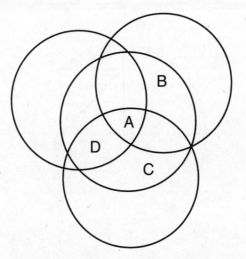

44. Look at the strip below, which has been made by taking a rectangular strip of paper, turning over one end (twisting it 180°) and joining the ends. How many sides does it have?

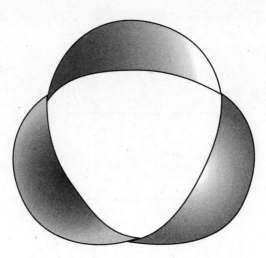

45. Given the dimensions of the radius in inches as shown in the diagram below, figure out the length of the rectangle's diagonal that goes from A to B.

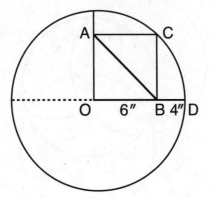

46. How can the following rectangle, with two jutting tabs, be cut into two pieces to make a complete rectangle?

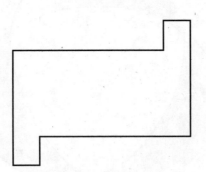

47. If two opposite corners of a checkerboard are removed, can the checkerboard be covered by dominoes, all like the one indicated? The size of each domino is the size of two adjacent squares of the checkerboard. The dominoes cannot be placed on top of each other and must lie flat.

Domino

48. An explorer decides, after a long day, to set up camp. She then walks one mile south from the camp, turns and walks one mile east. She turns again and walks one mile due north. At that point, she finds herself back where she started. How is that possible? Or, more precisely, where is that possible?

49. Assume that you have three and seven-ninths haystacks in one part of a field and two and two-thirds haystacks in another part. How many haystacks will you have if you put all the haystacks together?

50. A train leaves New York for Chicago traveling at the rate of 120 miles an hour. Another train leaves Chicago for New York an hour later traveling at the rate of 100 miles per hour. When the two trains meet (pass each other), which one is nearer to New York?

3

LOGICAL THINKING

From a drop of water a logician could infer the
possibility of an Atlantic or a Niagara without
having seen or heard of one or the other.
SIR ARTHUR CONAN DOYLE

EVELOPING THE ABILITY TO THINK LOGICALLY IS A PREREQUISITE for solving puzzles in mathematics, in science or even in life, for that matter. The great English puzzlist Henry E. Dudeney went so far as to claim that: "The history of puzzles entails nothing short of the actual story of the beginnings and development of exact thinking in man." The laws of logic form a system of thinking that is not unlike the grammar of a language. As a matter of fact, the word *logic* comes from the ancient Greek noun *lógos,* which means both "word" and "thought."

Thus, it comes as little surprise to find that the same areas of the brain involved in the processing of language, located primarily in the left hemisphere, are also activated when logical thinking is involved. The brain is a logical organ, someone once said—although, as you have already discovered in previous chapters, it is also a creative organ. Exercising that organ systematically with logic puzzles can only be of benefit.

IQ LOGIC

If you have ever taken an IQ test, then you may be familiar with this type of puzzle. The number in the center of each puzzle is the result of an operation (or operations)—such as addition or subtraction—carried out on the numbers in the four corners (in some way, in some order). All you have to do is figure out what the missing number in the last grid is by logically observing the previous grids, including the relationship and the placement of the numbers in them. While the puzzles start off fairly easy, some of them are really hard and you may need to use a lot of trial and error.

1. The number 10 in the center of the first grid is the result of some operation having been performed on the corner numbers 3, 2, 4, 1.

3		2
	10	
4		1

3		4
	43	
15		21

12		6
	29	
2		9

4		6
	?	
1		27

2.

2		1
	24	
3		4

4		3
	96	
4		2

8		3
	48	
1		2

5		2
	?	
2		4

3.

1		2
	12	
6		3

5		2
	28	
14		7

3		5
	32	
16		8

9		1
	?	
20		10

4.

2		8
	30	
4		16

1		4
	15	
2		8

6		24
	90	
12		48

3		12
	?	
6		24

5.

15		16
	19	
18		17

3		4
	7	
6		5

12		13
	16	
15		14

9		10
	?	
12		11

6.

9		5
	7	
6		8

12		8
	10	
9		11

18		14
	16	
15		17

22		18
	?	
19		21

7.

3		2
	18	
1		3

2		10
	44	
4		8

3		5
	30	
4		1

5		4
	?	
2		9

8.

2		5
	45	
4		3

6		4
	64	
4		2

9		4
	90	
5		1

3		6
	?	
1		4

9.

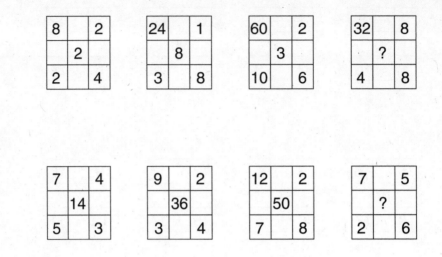

10.

DEDUCTION PUZZLES

The logic used to solve the sequences above involved searching for some connection in a given set of facts. Another type of logic, *deductive reasoning,* involves reaching a conclusion from premises or given facts. The conclusion is true if the premises or facts are true. Thus, if it is agreed that all puzzle solvers love puzzles and that Sarah is a puzzle solver, then it can logically be concluded that Sarah loves puzzles. It may or may not be true in real life, but it is a logical conclusion nonetheless.

The following is a classic puzzle in this genre—actually, it's the first one ever invented by Henry Dudeney. Only the names and professions have been changed. Let's go through it together.

✸ Sample Deduction Puzzle

In a certain company, the positions of CEO, analyst and accountant are held by Alex, Sheila and Sarah, but not necessarily in that order. The accountant, who is an only child, earns the least. Sarah, who is married to Alex's brother, earns more than the analyst. What position does each person fill?

The first thing to do is draw a cell chart, putting the positions—CEO, analyst, accountant—on one axis and the names of the persons—Alex, Sheila, Sarah—on the other. This allows you to keep track of all the deductions made along the way. For the sake of convenience, the cell charts are provided for the puzzles in this section.

	CEO	Analyst	Accountant
Alex			
Sheila			
Sarah			

We are told that: (1) the accountant is an only child, and (2) Alex has a brother (to whom, incidentally, Sarah is married). What can we deduce from these two facts? Clearly, we can eliminate Alex as the accountant, as he is not an only child. We show this by placing an *X* in the cell opposite his name under the column headed *Accountant*. This indicates that this possibility is eliminated for Alex.

	CEO	Analyst	Accountant
Alex			X
Sheila			
Sarah			

We are also told that the accountant earns the least of the three and that Sarah earns more than the analyst. From these facts, two obvious things about Sarah can be established: (1) she is not the accountant (who earns the least, while she earns more than someone else) and (2) she is not the analyst (for she earns more than he or she does). To keep track of these two conclusions, we enter two *X*s in their appropriate cells, eliminating accountant and analyst as possibilities for Sarah.

	CEO	Analyst	Accountant
Alex			X
Sheila			
Sarah		X	X

Now, look closely at the chart. Do you see that the only cell left vacant under *Accountant* is opposite Sheila? By the process of elimination, Sheila is the accountant. We show this by putting an *O* opposite her name in the cell and eliminating all other possibilities for her with *X*s, because Sheila can hold only one of the stated positions—if she is the accountant, then, logically, she is neither the CEO nor the analyst.

	CEO	Analyst	Accountant
Alex			X
Sheila	X	X	O
Sarah		X	X

The chart above now shows that Sarah is the CEO, since the only cell left vacant for her is under the heading *CEO*. We show this with an *O*. This eliminates the CEO possibility for Alex as well, since there is only one CEO. We show this with an *X*.

	CEO	Analyst	Accountant
Alex	X		X
Sheila	X	X	O
Sarah	O	X	X

The only cell left vacant for Alex is under *Analyst*.

	CEO	Analyst	Accountant
Alex	X	O	X
Sheila	X	X	O
Sarah	O	X	X

In summary, the chart helped us do two important things: (1) keep track of the deductions we made, and (2) show us further deductions that could be made as we went along. ❁

The first few puzzles in this set are really simple. They get progressively more complicated, although not necessarily harder. Cell charts are provided throughout, as are summary charts at the end, which you might want to use to keep track of what you are deducing as you go along. These might seem superfluous for the early puzzles, but they will definitely come in handy for the later ones.

11. The Vera family members—father, mother and four-year-old daughter—use nicknames with each other—Bee, Cat and Wee—but not necessarily in that order. Bee is not the father, and Bee is older than Wee (a female). How are the three related to each other?

	Bee	Cat	Wee
father			
mother			
daughter			

Relation	Nickname
father	
mother	
daughter	

12. Ms. Violet, Ms. Scarlet and Ms. Brown were having dinner together the other night to celebrate Ms. Scarlet's birthday. One of the three wore a violet skirt, another wore a scarlet skirt and the third wore a brown skirt. Interestingly, none of the colors of the skirts matched the names. Ms. Violet sat next to someone who wore a brown skirt. Can you determine the color of each woman's skirt?

	violet	scarlet	brown
Ms. Violet			
Ms. Scarlet			
Ms. Brown			

Name	Skirt color
Ms. Violet	
Ms. Scarlet	
Ms. Brown	

13. Four friends got a cat and a dog each last week. Each one decided to name his or her cat after the dog of one of the others. The dogs have different names. Can you determine the names of the cats and dogs? You will only need a summary chart for this puzzle.

1. One of the dogs is named Mack.
2. Harry's cat is not named Benji.
3. Harry's dog is named Ruff.
4. Danny's cat is named Droopy.
5. Gina named her cat after Barbara's dog.

Friend	Cat	Dog
Gina		
Barbara		
Harry		
Danny		

14. Becky, Pat, Rina and Sam are musicians. One is a drummer, one a pianist, one a singer and one a violinist, although not necessarily in that order. What is each person's musical field?

1. Becky and Rina attended the singer's recital last night.
2. Pat and the violinist always go to the recitals of their common friend, the pianist.
3. The violinist often performs with Sam and Becky.
4. Becky does not always get along with the pianist.

	drummer	pianist	singer	violinist
Becky				
Pat				
Rina				
Sam				

Name	Field
Becky	
Pat	
Rina	
Sam	

15. Five women and one man, including a profiler, were invited to a crime scene in a large precinct as experts. Can you determine each person's area of expertise?

1. Katia, Lina and the anthropologist met at the airport as they came in.
2. Paul, the only male in the group, is not the criminologist.
3. Maya is not the detective.
4. Johanna is neither the anthropologist nor the DNA expert.
5. After viewing the crime scene, the six experts had a general discussion about the crime at lunch together. Sitting around the table were the criminologist, Katia, Johanna, the weapons expert, the female detective and Pina.

	profiler	anthro-pologist	crimi-nologist	detective	DNA	weapons
Katia						
Lina						
Maya						
Johanna						
Pina						
Paul						

Name	Area of Expertise
Katia	
Lina	
Maya	
Johanna	
Pina	
Paul	

16. Four friends decided to enroll in four separate courses, including fencing. Which course did each one take?

1. Sandhu didn't take ballet or judo.
2. Neither Hanna nor Amin enrolled in ballet.
3. Either Laura or Amin took the opera course.

	opera	ballet	fencing	judo
Sandhu				
Hanna				
Laura				
Amin				

Name	Course
Sandhu	
Hanna	
Laura	
Amin	

17. Indira placed items into her briefcase in a specific order. Can you determine the order in which she did so? This puzzle is much harder than it appears, but all the information you need to know is given.

1. She placed an item inside just before putting in the cell phone and just after putting in the SMS device.
2. She put in the notepad just before putting in her keys.
3. She did not put the earphones in second.

	keys	notepad	ear	cell	SMS
First					
Second					
Third					
Fourth					
Fifth					

Order	Item
First	
Second	
Third	
Fourth	
Fifth	

18. Vanessa has taught four different instruments, including the saxophone, in different conservatories. Incredibly, she has taught each instrument in a different city and in a different year, from 2006 through 2009. See if you can figure out the year in which she taught a specific instrument and in what city she taught it.

 As in the case of puzzle 13, only a summary chart is provided. If you need a cell chart as well, just make one up by yourself. It's easy to do.

1. Vanessa taught the trumpet at least two years after she taught in Milwaukee.
2. In 2008, she taught in Atlanta.
3. She taught in Orlando before teaching the clarinet.
4. The instrument she taught in Denver and the one she taught in 2007 were the clarinet and the horn, although not necessarily in that order.

Year	Instrument	City
2006		
2007		
2008		
2009		

The last two puzzles in this genre will be a lot more complicated. For each of them, you will find three sets of facts. For example, in puzzle 19 you are given: (1) the names of certain people, (2) the colors of their iPods and (3) the beverages they ordered.

 In puzzles 13 and 18, you have already solved puzzles with three sets of facts. In those puzzles, however, summary charts were provided. In the next two puzzles, cell charts are provided. To correlate three sets in a cell chart, you will need to repeat one of them to the right of and under another set. This makes it possible to register correlations among the sets simultaneously.

19. Bella, Chita, Ira, Dina and Mika are the best of friends. Yesterday, they met at a café to compare their new iPods. Each iPod was a different color (black, blue, green, red, orange), and each friend ordered a different beverage (coffee, soft drink, juice, milk, tea). What color iPod did each person have, and what beverage did each one order?

1. The person with the red iPod ordered the soft drink.
2. Chita had the juice.
3. Dina brought a blue iPod.
4. Mika did not order milk.
5. The person who ordered milk had the orange iPod.
6. Bella had a green iPod. She did not order the coffee.

		iPod Color					Beverage Ordered				
		black	blue	green	red	orange	coffee	soft	juice	milk	tea
N	Bella										
a	Chita										
m	Ira										
e	Dina										
s	Mika										
B	coffee										
e	soft										
v	juice										
s	milk										
	tea										

repeated set

Name	iPod Color	Beverage Ordered
Bella		
Chita		
Ira		
Dina		
Mika		

20. Amy, Katia, Shamila, Renata and Henrietta work as store clerks at a large mall. One of them has the last name of Miller. Each woman sells only one kind of merchandise. From the following clues, determine each woman's full name and what she sells.

1. Renata, who does not know Ms. Kristoff, does not sell jewelry.
2. Ms. Armad does not sell CDs or books.
3. The five women are Shamila, Renata, Ms. Smith, Ms. Cramer and the clothing salesperson.
4. Amy's last name is neither Kristoff nor Cramer. Neither Amy nor Ms. Cramer sells CDs.
5. Neither the computer clerk nor the clothing salesperson is named Henrietta or Ms. Armad.

		Last Names				Items				
		Cramer	Armad	Miller	Smith	Kristoff	CDs	clothes	com- puters	jewels	books
N	Amy										
a	Katia										
m	Shamila										
e	Renata										
s	Henrietta										
I	CDs										
t	clothes										
e	computers										
m	jewels										
s	books										

repeated set

First Name	Last Name	Item Sold
Amy		
Katia		
Shamila		
Renata		
Henrietta		

As their name implies, logical comparison puzzles require you to compare things, people, events and so on to derive an appropriate conclusion or set of conclusions from them. That's all there is to it. The puzzles start off very easy to get you into the groove for the later and harder puzzles.

21. Maria, who is taller than Juan, is shorter than Jack. Deb is shorter than Juan. Who's the tallest of the four?

22. Bill earns more than two of his three friends—Shauna, Maggie and Betty. Betty does not earn the most, while Maggie earns less than Betty. Who earns the most and the least?

23. Jack, Jessie, Mack, Mary and Xavier were in a five-person race. Jack came in ahead of two runners but behind the other two. Xavier came in right after Mack, and Jessie came in right after Mary. Mary came in after Xavier. Who won the race?

24. In another race, Betty beat Cheryl, and Meagan beat Sandy. Kathy came in right after Sandy. Mary came in right after Kathy but ahead of Betty. Who won the race?

25. Six friends are all of different heights. Louise is shorter than Lucy, Danielle is shorter than Chris and Sarah is shorter than Alex. Lucy and Chris are shorter than Sarah. Lucy is shorter than Danielle. Who's the tallest and the shortest?

26. Six friends have names that start with the first six letters of the alphabet—Aaron, Barney, Cheryl, Dina, Evelyn and Frank. All are of varying heights. Their heights do not correspond alphabetically—that is, Aaron, whose name starts with the letter *A*, is not the tallest of the group; Barney, whose name starts with the letter *B*, is not the second tallest of the group; and so on. Those whose names start with the first three letters (*A, B, C*) are the shortest. Barney is shorter than Cheryl, but taller than Aaron. Also, Dina is shorter than Frank, but taller than Evelyn. Who's the tallest of the group?

27. In a poetry-writing contest, the contestants were required to use only the first ten letters of the alphabet—*A, B, C, D, E, F, G, H, I, J*—with which to start their words. The poems were collected and analyzed. Strangely, no one used *A* or *J*. Of the remaining letters, three were used the most. These three were earlier in the alphabetic sequence than two other letters, but later in the sequence than three other letters. Of these three letters, the one most used was alphabetically the first. What was the most frequently used letter?

28. Five boys and five girls took the same test. The girls' names started with the five vowels—*A, E, I, O, U*. The boys' names started with the first five consonants, alphabetically speaking—*B, C, D, F, G*. Here are the results of the test. The top five scorers consisted of two girls and three boys. The names of the top five started with letters that were in alphabetic sequence. The top scorer was a girl. Her name did not start with *A*. With what letter did her name begin?

29. Here's a "mind twister," as it can be called (in parallel to a tongue twister). Jack is taller than Jill, who's shorter than Jen, who's shorter than Jack, who's shorter than Jeb. Who is the tallest?

30. Here's one more mind twister for you. Mack is taller than Hack, who's shorter than Dack, who's shorter than Jack, who's shorter than Zack. Who is the shortest?

LIAR PUZZLES

In the 1930s, the British puzzlist Hubert Phillips (1891–1964) added an interesting category to the logic puzzles genre, which can be called, simply, liar puzzles. Phillips was known among his readers as "Caliban," the monstrous figure in Shakespeare's play *The Tempest*. Let's go through his original puzzle together. Only the names and circumstances have been changed.

✹ Sample Liar Puzzle

The people of an advanced and sophisticated island culture belong to one of two tribes, the Bali or the Mali. The members speak a common language. It is known, moreover, that the members of the Bali tribe always tell the truth, no matter what the situation, whereas the members of the Mali tribe always lie in the presence of strangers as a defensive strategy. An anthropologist, a stranger to the island culture, interviewed three islanders. "To which tribe do you belong?" the anthropologist asked the first. "Dorna," replied the islander in his native language. "What did he say?" asked the anthropologist of the second and third individuals, who answered her in English. "He said that he is a Bali," said the second. "No, he said that he is a Mali," countered the third. To which tribes do the second and third individuals belong?

Here's how to reason this out. There are two possibilities for the first speaker: either he is a Bali or he is a Mali. Let's assume that he is a Bali—the tribe whose members always tell the truth. In answer to the anthropologist's question "To which tribe do you belong?" he would have said, truthfully, "I am a Bali." So the translation of "Dorna" in this case is "I am a Bali."

Let's assume he is a Mali—the tribe whose members always lie in the presence of strangers. In answer to the anthropologist's question "To which tribe do you belong?" he would not have said, truthfully, "I am a Mali." He would have lied and said instead, "I am a Bali." So the translation of "Dorna" in this case is also "I am a Bali."

The second one thus spoke the truth in answer to the anthropologist's question "What did he say?" So the second native is a Bali. The third one obviously lied. So the third native is a Mali.

By the way, it is obviously not possible to determine to which tribe the first one actually belonged.

The first five puzzles in this section take place in a village where there are two clans. The members of one clan always tell the truth and those of the other always lie in the presence of those who do not belong to the village. Again, this is a defensive strategy. ✹

31. My sister, a logician, visited the village a while back. She ran into a man and a woman walking together. She asked the woman, "Are you a truth-teller?" "Goneh," she replied in her native language. My sister then asked the man what the woman had said. "She said 'no,'" was his reply in English. To which clan did the man belong?

32. The day after, my brother, a lawyer, also paid the village a visit. He also ran into two people from the village, a woman and a man. He asked the woman, "Are you a truth-teller?" "Goneh," she replied. My brother then asked the man what she had said. He replied in English, "She said 'yes,' but she is a liar." To which clan(s) did both my brother's informants belong?

33. A week ago, my cousin, a sociologist, interviewed three members of the village. The truth-speaking people are called Tamis, and members of the clan who lie strategically are called Famis. He asked one of them, "To what clan do you belong?" The villager answered, "Buneh." My cousin then asked the other two, "What did he say?" "He said he was a Tami, but he lied," said the second villager in English. "No, he said he was a Fami," said the third, also in English. To which clan did each villager belong?

34. My cousin then decided to interview three other villagers. To the first one, he posed the question "Are you a Fami?" The villager's answer was muffled and could not be understood. So my cousin asked the other two, "What did she say?" "She said she was not a Fami," answered the second villager. "No, she didn't," replied the third, "my partner just lied to you." To which clan did each villager belong?

35. This time, my husband decided to interview three villagers. He asked only the first one: "Are your two partners both Tamis?" The villager answered, "Yes, they are, even though they will not admit it." On the basis of that answer alone, determine to which clans the three villagers belonged.

There are other types of puzzles that involve lying or false statements. Some have ancient origins, such as the so-called Liar Paradox. The remaining puzzles in this section present you with a few of these different types.

36. Here's the original Liar Paradox. The Cretan philosopher Epimenides once said: "All Cretans are liars." Did Epimenides speak the truth?

37. The second-most famous paradox of this kind, after the Liar Paradox (puzzle 36), was formulated by British philosopher Bertrand Russell (1872–1970). In a small village, a barber shaves everyone who does not shave himself. Does he shave himself? Incidentally, this puzzle has come to be known as the Barber Paradox.

38. Let's add a follow-up from the village of puzzles 31–35 into this mix. Is it possible for anyone to make the following statement: "All the members of my village are liars"?

39. Last week, I bought a jewelry box at an antique sale. The box bears the following inscription:

> This box was not made by a liar.

Was the box made by a truth-teller or a liar?

RAYMOND SMULLYAN

The master creator of liar puzzles is the American logician Raymond Smullyan (b. 1919), whose many puzzle books are as delightful as they are challenging. His book titled *What's the Name of This Book?* is a veritable tour de force in the liar puzzle genre.

40. A rare gold coin is in one of the following three boxes. Each one has an inscription written on it:

A	B	C
The coin is in here.	The coin is not in here.	The coin is not in A.

Can you tell where the coin is if, at most, only one of the inscriptions is true?

The last set of puzzles involves, yet again, a different kind of truth-liar logic. They are called simply truth puzzles or Who Dunnit? puzzles. These puzzles highlight the role of consistency—or the fact that a set of statements must not yield contradictory conclusions—in logical thinking. Let's go through one together.

⊛ Sample Truth Puzzle

Jake, Bill and Sonny were brought in by the police yesterday because one of them was suspected of having stolen some money. The three suspects made the following statements under intense questioning:

JAKE: **I'm innocent.**

BILL: **I'm innocent.**

SONNY: **Bill is the guilty one.**

If only one of these statements turned out to be true, who stole the money? A truth chart, such as the one below, can help us determine who the culprit was.

	Statement	Truth Value
Jake	I'm innocent.	
Bill	I'm innocent.	
Sonny	Bill is the guilty one.	

For the sake of convenience, let T = a true statement and F = a false statement. We are told that only one of the three statements turned out to be true. This means that one T and two Fs were uttered yesterday.

Bill's statement ("I'm innocent") and Sonny's statement ("Bill is the guilty one") contradict each other. So one is true (T) and the other false (F). No other logical conclusion can be drawn from these two statements taken together. Let's assume that Bill's statement is the false one and Sonny's the true one.

	Statement	Truth Value
Jake	I'm innocent.	
Bill	I'm innocent.	F
Sonny	Bill is the guilty one.	T

Under the condition that there were one true statement and two false ones, Jake's statement must be the other false one. Let's assign it an F-value.

	Statement	Truth Value
Jake	I'm innocent.	F
Bill	I'm innocent.	F
Sonny	Bill is the guilty one.	T

Now, consider the logical outcome of this arrangement. Jake's statement has an F-value, so he was the guilty party. Why? Because he said, "I'm innocent," but that statement is false. If he's not innocent, then he's guilty. Bill said that he too was innocent. According to the chart, his statement is also false. By the same reasoning, he too was guilty. But there was only one robber. Obviously, this is an inconsistency.

What to do? We reject the initial hypothesis—that Sonny told the truth and Bill lied. But not all was a waste of our time. In the process, we learned that Sonny's statement was false and, thus, that Bill told the truth—the reverse of our initial assumption.

	Statement	Truth Value
Jake	I'm innocent.	
Bill	I'm innocent.	T
Sonny	Bill is the guilty one.	F

Because there was only one true statement (made by Bill), Jake's statement turns out to be false again.

	Statement	Truth Value
Jake	I'm innocent.	F
Bill	I'm innocent.	T
Sonny	Bill is the guilty one.	F

Now, since Jake's statement ("I'm innocent") is false, it can be concluded that he was the robber. Bill's statement ("I'm innocent") can now be seen to be true, as correctly indicated by the T-value opposite his statement. And Sonny's statement ("Bill is the guilty one") can be seen to be false, as is indicated by the F-value opposite his statement.

Since there are no inconsistencies, we have deduced that Jake is the one who stole the money. ✹

Now it's your turn. If you need a truth chart in the process of solving the following puzzles, you can create one by following the model in the sample puzzle.

41. Three boys, Andrew, Zack and Chris, were caught eating a pie stolen from a bakery. One of them stole it alone and then shared it with his two friends. The three boys were interrogated by the shop owner. The boy who stole the pie is the one who made a false statement, while the other two boys made true statements. Here are three statements, in no particular order. Who stole the pie?

Andrew: Chris did it.

Zack: Andrew's statement is false.

Chris: Zack's statement is true.

42. Someone robbed a computer shop yesterday. Four suspects were rounded up and interrogated. One of them was indeed the robber. Here's what they said under police questioning:

Arthur: Daniel did it.

Daniel: Tug did it.

Garth: I didn't do it.

Tug: Daniel lied when he said that I did it.

Only one of these four statements turned out to be true. Who was the guilty man?

43. Four women, one of whom was known to have stolen a car, were brought in by the police the morning after the theft. The four suspects made the same pattern of statements when interrogated by the lead detective on the case as did the previous suspects:

Amelia: Doreen did it.

Doreen: Tamara did it.

Genelle: I didn't steal it.

Tamara: Doreen lied when she said I stole it.

This time, however, only one of these statements turned out to be false—all the others were true. Who stole the car?

44. Mack the Nat was found murdered one night in a back alley. The next day, the police rounded up three suspects, who were interrogated by the toughest detective around, Martha Jones. The suspects made the following statements to her:

Bubba: 1. I didn't kill Mack.

2. Jason is not my friend.

3. I knew Mack.

Jason: 1. I didn't kill Mack.

2. Bubba and Marooney are friends of mine.

3. Bubba didn't kill Mack.

Marooney: 1. I didn't kill Mack.

2. Bubba lied when he said that Jason was not his friend.

3. I don't know who killed Mack.

Only one of the three is guilty, and only one of each man's three statements is false, the other two being true. Who killed Mack the Nat?

45. Horatio, a notorious biker, was killed last night. Four suspects were quickly rounded up and brought in for questioning. Here's what they said under interrogation:

Al: Either Ben or Cam did it.

Ben: Yeah, I killed him. He had it coming.

Cam: Nah, Ben didn't do it. Dick did.

Dick: I did not. Al killed Horatio.

Only one suspect told the truth, and the other three lied. Who killed Horatio?

46. Four teens were called into the principal's office, suspected of having taken a teacher's car keys out of mischief. In fact, only one of them did it. But each made a statement to the principal.

Everett:	I admit it. I did it.
Frank:	Yeah, either Everett stole the keys or I did so.
Gill:	Nah, you're all wrong. Horace is the guy.
Horace:	No way! Frank did it.

Only one spoke the truth. All the others lied. Who took the car keys?

47. Five suspects were rounded up after Billy was killed. They made the following statements, of which all but one were true. The false one was made by the killer. Who killed Billy?

Andy:	I didn't do it.
Benny:	Carson did it.
Carson:	I didn't do it.
Darcy:	Eckhardt didn't do it.
Eckhardt:	Benny spoke the truth.

48. Billy's friend, also a member of an unsavory group, was killed shortly after Billy was. Five suspects were again brought in. Only one was the killer, and he made the only true statement. The others, for some reason, all lied. Who killed Billy's friend?

Nat:	Kat did it.
Pat:	Jat didn't do it.
Bat:	Nat did it.
Kat:	Bat did it.
Jat:	Pat lied.

49. The last member of Billy's group was also killed. Another five suspects were brought in. Only one of them was the killer. He spoke the truth, as did one other person. The three others lied. Who was the killer?

Ack: Beck did it.

Beck: Drew didn't do it.

Crew: I did it.

Drew: Ack did it.

Evan: Nah, I did it.

50. The last puzzle is a truly tricky one, written by famed puzzlist Boris Kordemsky for the journal *Scripta Mathematica*. Get your thinking caps on. This is a classic!

    The purse of an elementary school teacher in New York was stolen. The thief had to be Lillian, Judy, David, Theo or Margaret. When questioned, each child made three statements.

Lillian: 1. I didn't take the purse.

            2. I have never in my life stolen anything.

            3. Theo did it.

Judy: 4. I didn't take the purse.

            5. My daddy is rich enough, and I have a purse of my own.

            6. Margaret knows who did it.

David: 7. I didn't take the purse.

            8. I didn't know Margaret before I enrolled in this school.

            9. Theo did it.

Theo: 10. I am not guilty.

            11. Margaret did it.

            12. Lillian is lying when she says I stole the purse.

Margaret: 13. I didn't take the teacher's purse.

            14. Judy is guilty.

            15. David can vouch for me because he has known me since I was born.

Later, each child admitted that two of his or her statements were true and one was false. Assuming this is true, who stole the purse?

4
REASONING

Either you think, or else others have to think
for you and take power from you.
F. SCOTT FITZGERALD

EASONING, AS THE WORD SUGGESTS, involves the ability to analyze the best way to do
something—such as arranging or organizing—or what pattern is hidden in a set of
facts. The puzzles in this chapter require you to activate your reasoning skills in a
focused manner. Reasoning is, primarily, a left-hemisphere function. However, the puzzles
here are not as straightforward as were the logic puzzles of the previous chapter—which
also involved reasoning of specific kinds. These are distinguished from them in requiring a
little bit of insight, a mental activity that entails the use of right-hemisphere functions. In
short, these puzzles will activate your brain as a whole, especially the so-called "association
cortex"—the area that controls how we combine information stored in memory with information gathered by the senses.

In a classic study published in 1982, the psychologists Robert J. Sternberg and Janet E.
Davidson investigated the relationship between puzzle solving and IQ. They found that the
capacity to use reasoning and insight thinking in tandem to solve puzzles did not always
correlate with IQ, but did nonetheless benefit a large cross-section of people intellectually.
So let's get to it.

DRAWING AND WEIGHING PUZZLES

The puzzles in this section involve systematic reasoning about drawing things out of boxes or weighing things on scales. These are classics. In other puzzle books, these might be classified under different rubrics. They are included here, however, simply because they are based on a specific pattern or principle and thus involve a specific kind of reasoning combined with a touch of insight.

1. In a box, there are twenty balls, ten white and ten black. They all have the same indistinguishable texture to them. With a blindfold on, what is the least number of balls you must draw out of the box to be sure of having a pair of balls that matches in color—two white or two black? That is, you cannot assume luck—drawing out two white balls or two black balls in a row. You must remove enough balls to guarantee a color match, even if you have some left over, when you take your blindfold off.

2. Now, let's increase the number of balls in the box to thirty—ten white, ten black and ten green. What is the least number of balls you must draw out of the box this time (with a blindfold on, of course) to be sure of having a pair of balls that matches in color—two white, two black or two green?

3. Let's increase the number of balls in the box again to forty—ten white, ten black, ten green and ten red. With your blindfold back on, what is the least number of balls you must draw out of the box this time to be sure of having a pair of balls that matches in color—two white, two black, two green or two red? Moreover, can you see a general pattern emerging from having solved three puzzles of this type?

4. Let's increase the number one more time to fifty, but this time let's vary the number of colored ball sets. In the box, there are two white, eighteen black, sixteen green, four red and ten orange balls. Again, what is the least number of balls you must draw out of the box this time (blindfolded) to be sure of having a pair of balls that matches in color—two white, two black, two green, two red or two orange? Does the new proportion of balls affect the outcome?

5. If there are six pairs of black gloves and six pairs of white gloves in a box, all mixed up, what is the least number of draws that are required, with a blindfold on, to guarantee a matching pair of black or white gloves? In this case, a pair consists of one left-hand and one right-hand glove of the same color.

6. Let's change the situation a bit again. In a box, there are thirteen balls—six white, four black and three blue. With a blindfold on, what is the least number of balls you must draw out to get three matching balls—three white, three black or three blue?

7. I have six billiard balls, one of which weighs less than the other five. They all look the same. How can I identify the one that weighs less on a balance scale with only two weighings?

8. I now have seven billiard balls, one of which weighs less than the other six. They all look the same. What is the least number of weighings I will need to identify the one that weighs less on a balance scale?

9. This time I have twelve billiard balls, one of which weighs less than the other eleven. They all look the same. What is the least number of weighings I will need to identify the one that weighs less on a balance scale?

10. This time I have twenty-one balls, one of which weighs less than the other twenty. What is the least number of weighings on a balance scale that I will need to identify the one that weighs less?

MOVEMENT AND CROSSING PUZZLES

Puzzles involving coins, balls and so on that are to be moved in a certain way and puzzles that involve crossing a river under given circumstances have been around since time immemorial. All require the use of clever reasoning. The puzzles here include some real classics.

11. Let's start off really simple. There are two checkers in a row on a table, one white and one black, with one space between the two.

Switch the positions of the checkers by moving only one checker at a time.

A checker may be moved over one adjacent checker into an empty space, or it may be moved one space into an empty space. You are not allowed to move a checker backward; that is, the white one can only move to the right and the black one only to the left.

12. Let's make the puzzle a little harder. This time, there are four checkers in a row on a table, two white and two black, with one space between the two colors.

Switch the positions of the checkers by moving only one checker at a time.

As before, a checker may be moved over one adjacent checker into an empty space, or else it may be moved one space into an empty space. You are not allowed to move a checker backward: that is, the white ones can only move to the right, and the black ones to the left.

13. Let's make the puzzle harder still. Now there are six checkers in a row on a table, three white and three black, with one space between the two sets.

As before, switch the positions of the checkers by moving only one checker at a time.

A checker may be moved over one adjacent checker into an empty space or else it may be moved one space into an empty space. You are not allowed to move a checker backward; that is, white checkers can only move to the right, and black ones to the left.

14. There are twelve coins on a table arranged as shown:

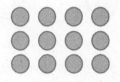

Six squares can be discerned in this arrangement, as shown:

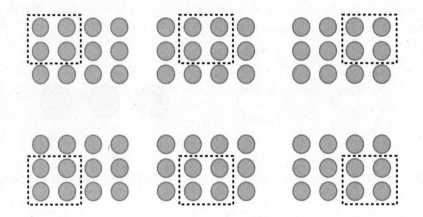

Remove three coins to leave three equal squares.

15. A traveler comes to a riverbank with a wolf, a goat and a head of cabbage. To his chagrin, he notes that there is only one boat for crossing over, which can carry no more than two passengers—the traveler and either one of the two animals or the cabbage. As the traveler knows, if left alone together, the goat will eat the cabbage and the wolf will eat the goat. The wolf does not eat cabbage. How does the traveler transport his animals and his cabbage to the other side intact in a minimum number of back-and-forth trips?

16. Three wives and their husbands come to a river. The small boat that will take them across holds only two people. To avoid any compromising situations, the crossings are to be so arranged that no woman shall be left alone with a man unless her husband is present. If any man or woman can be the rower, how many crossings are required?

ALCUIN

Charlemagne (742–814 CE), the founder of the Holy Roman Empire, apparently became so obsessed over puzzles that he hired an expert to create them for his enjoyment.

The person he selected for the job was the famous English scholar and ecclesiastic Alcuin (732–804 CE). The resourceful Alcuin put the puzzles he invented for Charlemagne into an instructional manual, titled (in abbreviated form) *Propositiones ad acuendos juvenes* ("Problems to Sharpen the Young"), in an attempt to get medieval youth interested in mathematics.

Puzzles 15 and 16 used here come from that anthology. Number 16 originally involved three men with unmarried sisters. The one used here is a reformulation by the Italian mathematician Niccolò Fontana Tartaglia (c. 1499–1557). Versions of the wolf, goat and cabbage puzzle have been found in different cultures throughout the world (with different characters, animals, victuals, objects and the like), although it is not clear if they predate Alcuin's text.

17. As a final river-crossing puzzle, here is a modern classic from the pen of Boris Kordemsky. A detachment of soldiers must cross a river. The bridge is broken, and the river is deep. The officer in charge spots two boys playing in a rowboat by the shore. The boat is so tiny, however, that it can only hold two boys or one soldier. All the soldiers succeed in crossing the river in the boat. How?

Puzzles in which you have to figure out kinship relations—who's your father's brother's son, for example—are excellent stimuli for activating your reasoning skills. These puzzles start off very simply, allowing your brain to get used to this sort of convoluted thinking. The very last two puzzles, however, are classics in the genre.

18. A boy answers the phone. He asks, "Who's speaking?" The caller, a male, answers, "Don't you recognize me? Your mother's mother is my mother-in-law." Who is the caller?

19. A girl answers the phone. She asks, "Who's speaking?" The caller, a female, answers, "Don't you recognize me? Your father's sister's daughter is my own daughter." Who's the caller?

20. A man answers the phone this time. He asks, "Who's speaking?" The caller, a female, answers, "Don't you recognize me? Your father is my father-in-law." "Are you my aunt?" asks the man. "No, I am not," responds the female. Who's the caller?

21. A little girl answers the phone. She asks, "Who's speaking?" The caller, another little girl, answers, "Don't you recognize me? I'm your mother's sister's daughter." Who's the caller?

22. Who is your father's father's son?

23. Let's switch gender. Who is your mother's mother's daughter?

24. Who is your mother's father's son?

25. Who is your father's mother's daughter?

26. Who is your mother's sister's son?

27. Who is your wife's father's son?

28. Who is your husband's mother's daughter?

29. This puzzle is a classic from the pen of the great American puzzlist Sam Loyd (1841–1911). Uncle Reuben, who is unmarried, was in the big city to visit his sister, Mary Ann. They were walking together along a city street when they came to a small hotel. "Before we go any farther," Reuben said to his sister, "I should like to stop a moment and inquire about a sick nephew of mine who lives in this hotel." "Well," replied Mary Ann, "seeing as I don't happen to have any sick nephew to worry about, I will just trot on home. We can continue our sightseeing this afternoon." What relation was Mary Ann to the mysterious nephew?

30. This last one is from the pen of Henry E. Dudeney, and it never fails to stump people. A boy is looking at a photo: "Brothers and sisters have I none, but this man's son is my father's son." Who is the person in the picture?

One of the most vexing of all types of questions on IQ tests is the one that asks you to complete an analogy such as the following one:

Bird is to fly as human is to . . .

But such puzzles do provide a good mental workout. The answer, by the way, to the sample analogy is *walk*. Why? Because the analogy used involves the type of locomotion that is appropriate to a specific species: birds usually fly, while humans usually walk (and, of course, run, after they learn to walk). You will test your analogical reasoning skills in solving this next set of puzzles.

31. Pen is to paper as keyboard is to . . .

32. Boat is to water as airplane is to . . .

33. Love is to heart as thought is to . . .

34. House is to people as dam is to . . .

35. Sharp is to dull as bent is to . . .

36. Near is to close as distant is to . . .

37. Tulip is to flower as orange is to . . .

38. Frank is to Franca as Paul is to . . .

39. Words are to literature as figures are to . . .

40. Teachers are to classrooms as golfers are to . . .

41. Oxygen is to breathing as light is to . . .

42. Soft is to kindness as hard is to . . .

43. A is to B as one is to . . .

44. A is to Z as B is to . . .

45. Mister is to gentleman as madam is to . . .

46. Laughing is to happiness as crying is to . . .

47. Day is to birth as night is to . . .

MISCELLANEOUS REASONING PUZZLES

The last three puzzles in this chapter are all challenging, at least for many people. They involve pure reasoning, as you will see. And they are all classics in the genre. Good luck!

48. Three closed boxes are labeled A, B and C. One contains 10¢, one 15¢ and one 20¢ in nickels, but they are labeled incorrectly. Someone takes the money out of box B, which is labeled 15¢. Its contents, however, are two nickels. What are the contents of each box?

Box A	Box B	Box C
10¢	15¢	20¢

49. There are three boxes on a table: one with two black ties in it, the second one with two white ties in it and the third one with one black and one white tie. The boxes are labeled, logically enough, BB for two black ties, WW for two white ties and BW for one black and one white tie. Someone has switched the labels, so that each box is labeled incorrectly. Can you determine the contents of each box by drawing out only one tie?

To get you started, the possible contents of each box are displayed for you in the diagram below. As the diagram shows, each box will not contain the combination that its label says, but it could contain either of the other two combinations.

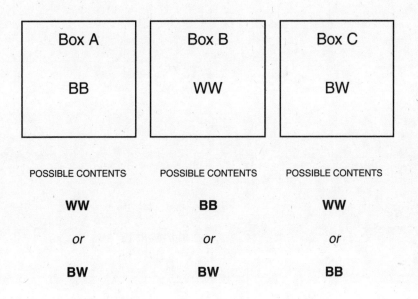

Box A	Box B	Box C
BB	WW	BW

POSSIBLE CONTENTS	POSSIBLE CONTENTS	POSSIBLE CONTENTS
WW	**BB**	**WW**
or	*or*	*or*
BW	**BW**	**BB**

50. Before they are blindfolded, three women are told that each one will have either a red or a blue cross painted on her forehead. When the blindfolds are removed, each woman is supposed to raise her hand if she sees a red cross and to drop her hand when she figures out the color of her own cross. The three women are blindfolded, and a red cross is drawn on each of their foreheads. The blindfolds are removed. After looking at each other, the three women raise their hands simultaneously. After a short time, one of the women lowers her hand and says, "My cross is red." How did she reason it out?

5
OUTSIDE-THE-BOX THINKING

*The moment of truth, the sudden emergence of
a new insight, is an act of intuition.*
ARTHUR KOESTLER

YOU MAY HAVE HEARD OF LATERAL THINKING. This term was introduced into psychology by Edward de Bono, a Maltese-born British psychologist. He coined it initially to refer to the use of one's thought processes in a nontraditional way—thinking "outside the box," as the expression goes. The term *lateral thinking* now encompasses a larger range of thinking processes, many of which you will find in the puzzles in this chapter.

The classic example of lateral thinking is the story about a truck stuck under a low bridge. As a group of people unsuccessfully tries to think of some way to force the truck out, a little boy, using lateral thinking, suggests that they deflate the tires.

This chapter will present you with puzzles that will challenge your logical thought processes. They will, in other words, force you to think outside the box. And they will definitely get your right hemisphere working overtime!

TRICK PUZZLES

Plays on words, tricks using number concepts and the like, all thrust your creative thinking processes into action. Many of these are classic puzzles that have, over the years, shown themselves to have a broad appeal. The likely reason is that they involve unraveling the hidden trick or ruse with which they are composed.

1. A bull is put on a scale. But he is so big that only three of his four legs will fit on the scale. The scale shows 1,000 pounds. How much do you estimate the bull weighs when he stands on all four legs?

2. In a stationery shop, the prices are set according to the clerk's whim. A pen costs $2.05, and a pad also costs $2.05. A pencil costs $4.10, and an agenda costs $3.15. How much does a calculator cost?

3. My brother has two current U.S. coins, which add up to 15¢. One of the two coins is not a nickel. What two coins does he have?

4. If it takes five minutes to boil an egg, how long will it take to boil five eggs?

5. Is it legal in the United States for a man to marry his widow's sister?

6. It takes twelve one-dollar stamps to make a dozen. How many two-dollar stamps does it take?

7. Three women decide to go on a holiday to Las Vegas. They share a room at a hotel that is charging 1920s rates as a promotional gimmick. The women are charged only $10 each, or $30 in all. After going through his guest list, the manager discovers that he has made a mistake and has overcharged the three vacationers. The room in which the three women are costs only $25. He gives a bellhop $5 to return to them. The sneaky bellhop knows that he cannot divide $5 into three equal amounts. Therefore, he pockets $2 for himself and returns only $1 to each woman. Here's the conundrum. Each woman paid $10 originally and got back $1, so each woman paid $9 for the room. The three of them together thus paid $9 x 3, or $27 in total. If we add this amount to the $2 that the bellhop dishonestly pocketed, we get a total of $29. Yet the women paid out $30 originally. Where is the other dollar?

8. After conducting several experiments, a professor of chemistry discovered that it took eighty minutes for a specific chemical reaction to occur when he was wearing his glasses, but that it took the same reaction an hour and twenty minutes to occur when he was not wearing them. Why?

9. Why are 1994 dollar bills worth more than 1984 dollar bills?

10. If you saw three shadows on three fence posts, one painted white, one painted blue and one painted red, which shadow would be the darkest?

11. How many times can you subtract the number one from the number twenty-five?

12. A farmer had seven daughters, and they each had a brother. How many children did he have?

13. This next puzzle is another version of the missing dollar one. Yesterday, in a suburban mall, the first customer in a bookstore gave the salesclerk a $10 bill for a $3 book. The bookstore was selling books at a barrel-bottom rate to make room for new ones. The salesclerk, having no change, took the $10 bill across the corridor to the record store to get it broken down into ten $1 bills. The salesclerk then gave the customer the book worth $3 and seven $1 bills as change. An hour later, the record-store salesclerk brought back the $10 bill, claiming that the bill was counterfeit and demanding her money back from the bookstore salesclerk. To avoid quarreling, the bookstore salesclerk decided to give her ten $1 bills, taking back the counterfeit one. What's the gist of the transactions that took place? The bookstore salesclerk was out $3 (the cost of the book), plus the ten $1 bills he gave to the record-store salesclerk. Altogether, he lost $13. But only $10 were used in the transactions. What happened?

14. Here's one more in this genre. It comes from pen of Lewis Carroll. Which clock keeps the best time, the clock that loses a minute a day or one that doesn't run at all?

INSIGHT THINKING PUZZLES

Eureka! You have likely heard this word and may even have used it yourself. It expresses triumph upon finding or discovering something through a sudden flash of insight. The word was supposedly uttered by Archimedes upon figuring out, in a flash of insight, how he could measure the volume of a solid and thus determine the purity of gold objects.

A similar English exclamation is "Aha!" Psychologists, in fact, often refer to insight thinking as "aha thinking," because it comes about seemingly spontaneously. The following puzzles will work on your aha thinking.

THE DOT PUZZLE

Puzzle 15 is the puzzle that gave origin to the expression "thinking outside the box." Around the middle of the twentieth century, people in business and education started referring to this puzzle as a prototypical example of what insight thinking is all about. It continues to be cited by psychologists as an example of how the mind tends to impose unnecessary limitations upon methods of addressing problems.

15. Without letting your pencil leave the paper, draw four straight lines through all of the following nine dots.

16. The nine-dot puzzle in puzzle 15 is a three-by-three version of what can be called generally a dot-joining puzzle. Next, solve the sixteen-dot (four-by-four) version. Again, you must connect the dots without lifting your pencil. How many lines are required in this case?

17. Try your hand at a twenty-five dot (five-by-five) version. Again, you must connect the dots without lifting your pencil. How many lines are required in this case?

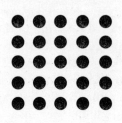

18. There are three cups and ten coins on a table.

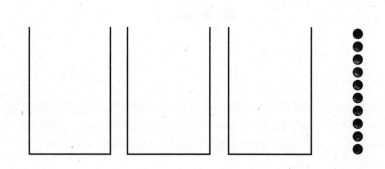

Put the coins in the three cups in such a way that the following conditions are met: (1) there is no empty cup, and (2) there must be seven coins in one cup and three in another. Is this possible?

19. The eminent mathematician Niccolò Tartaglia (c.1499–1557) was obviously frustrated by the fact that fractions don't always produce neat results. He came up with this classic puzzle in insight thinking. A man dies, leaving seventeen camels to be divided among his heirs, in the proportions one-half, one-third and one-ninth. How can this be done without killing the camels?

20. There are six oranges in a box. Without cutting up any of the oranges, my sister divided the six oranges among six friends, and yet one orange was left in the box. How did she do this?

21. Yesterday my brother withdrew $50 from his account at four times of the day, as shown:

$20	leaving	$30
$15	leaving	$15
$ 9	leaving	$ 6
$ 6	leaving	$ 0
——		——
$50		$51

Where did the extra dollar come from?

As mentioned at the start of this chapter, lateral thinking is a broad term covering a range of outside-the-box thinking processes. Here are a number of puzzles that clearly require that you use some of the lateral style of thinking. Some of these have elements of trick puzzles and others of insight puzzles.

22. How many times does the digit 4 appear in the numerals from 1 to 100?

23. What do you get if you cross a puddle and a pond?

24. Is it better to write an essay on an empty stomach or a full one?

25. How can you pull a rug out from under a desk if the desk is too heavy for you to lift?

26. Can you make six letters with three straight lines?

27. A banana is suspended from the ceiling just beyond your reach. Jumping won't help either—it is too high up. You are very hungry. How do you get the banana down?

28. You are driving late at night in a strange place and have become completely lost. As you drive along, you see a sign, but it has fallen down. What do you do?

29. Jack spent an hour at the doctor's office. He was not sick or injured, yet he had to be carried out of the office. Why?

30. How can you make four with three lines?

NUMERAL CONUNDRUMS

This next set of puzzles will really get your creative arithmetic juices flowing, as you will see. The puzzles are self-explanatory, so no introductory commentary is needed.

31. Use three fives to form an expression that equals six.

32. Use seven nines to form an expression that equals twelve.

33. Use only two nines to form an expression that equals twelve.

34. Use one nine only to form an expression that equals three.

35. Use three ones to form an expression that equals zero.

36. Use five twos to form an expression that equals two.

37. Use five Is to make a V.

38. Use a one and two zeroes to form one hundred.

39. Use a nine and a zero to form an expression that equals zero.

40. Use an I and a V to make four.

41. Use four twos to form an expression that equals one.

42. Use three twos to form an expression that equals two.

43. Use a four and a nine to form an expression that equals seven.

44. Use three letters to form 1.

MISCELLANEOUS PUZZLES

Some puzzles appear to have straightforward solutions, but they hide an unexpected twist or a hidden pattern. Some of these are like insight puzzles and thus tend to produce an aha reaction; others can be said to produce a "Ha, ha" one, since the joke is on the solver. Your final six outside-the-box puzzles fall into one or the other of these two categories.

45. This first puzzle is one of the oldest of this type. It has been found in manuscripts dating as far back as the early medieval ages. A snake is at the bottom of a 30-foot well. Each day it crawls up 3 feet and slips back 2 feet. The snake has the ability to stick to the walls of the well and thus does not slide down to the bottom at the end of a day when it stops to rest. At that rate, when will the snake be able to reach the top of the well?

46. Here's another classic in the genre. My dad decided to quit smoking after finishing the twenty-seven cigarettes he had left. Since it was my dad's habit to smoke only two-thirds of a cigarette at a time, he realized that he could reroll his butts into new cigarettes. If he smoked only once each day, how many days went by before he finally quit his bad habit?

47. Two children, a boy and a girl, were out riding their bikes yesterday, coming toward each other from opposite directions. When they were exactly twenty miles apart, they began racing toward each other. The instant they started, a fly on the handle of the girl's bike started flying toward the boy. As soon as it reached the handle on his bike, it turned around and flew back to the girl. The fly flew back and forth in this way, from handle bar to handle bar, until the two bicycles met. Each bike moved at a constant speed of ten miles per hour, and the swifter fly flew at a constant speed of fifteen miles an hour. How much total distance did the fly cover?

JOHN VON NEUMANN

If you were fooled into believing that puzzle 47 was more complicated than the solution given at the back, then you are in really exceptional company!

One of the greatest mathematicians of the twentieth century, the Hungarian-born John von Neumann (1903–1957) was a professor of mathematics at Princeton University. Among his many other accomplishments, his ideas led to the development of the modern computer. He was once asked to solve this very puzzle at a cocktail party.

Von Neumann thought about the puzzle for a moment and then gave the correct answer. The person who posed the puzzle to him was amazed, because he had always remarked that mathematicians constantly overlooked the simple way it can be solved, trying instead to solve it by a lengthy and complicated process using advanced mathematics (summing an infinite series).

Von Neumann looked surprised and retorted, matter-of-factly, "Well, that's precisely how I solved it!"

48. Three books, all the same width, are stacked upright against each other on a bookshelf. Each cover is a ½-inch thick, and the pages of each book are 2 inches thick. A bookworm starts on the first page of the book on the left and bores its way straight through to the last page of the book on the right. How far has the bookworm gone? Be very careful with this one!

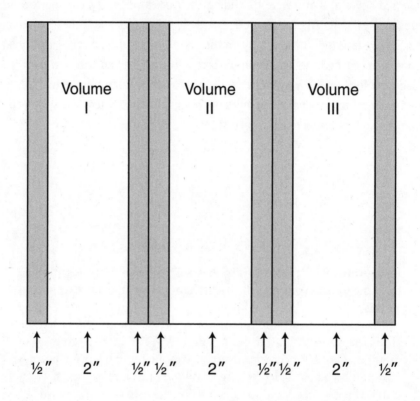

Volume I   Volume II   Volume III

↑ ½"   ↑ 2"   ↑ ½" ↑ ½"   ↑ 2"   ↑ ½" ↑ ½"   ↑ 2"   ↑ ½"

49. There are two containers on a table, A and B. A is half full with wine, while B, which is twice A's size, is one-quarter full with wine. Both containers are filled with water, and the contents are poured into a third container, C, which is large enough to hold the contents of both A and B. What proportion of container C's mixture is wine?

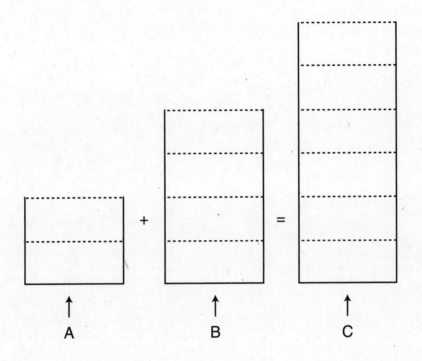

50. The last puzzle is actually an anecdote that refers to one of the greatest insight thinkers of all time, the German mathematician Carl Friedrich Gauss (1777–1855). The story goes that Gauss was only ten years old when he dazzled his teacher with his wizardry at arithmetical calculation. One day, his class was asked to cast the sum of all the numbers from one to one hundred: 1 + 2 + 3 + 4 + . . . + 100 = ? Amazingly, Gauss raised his hand within seconds and gave the correct response of 5,050, while the other students continued to toil over this seemingly endless arithmetical task. When the teacher asked him how he was able to come up with the answer so quickly, he gave a reply that revealed true aha thinking. What was it?

6
SUDOKU
AND OTHER PLACEMENT PUZZLES

*Logic takes care of itself; all we have to do
is to look and see how it does it.*
LUDWIG WITTGENSTEIN

I N 2005, "SUDOKUMANIA" TOOK OVER THE WORLD. That was the year when virtually every newspaper started carrying a Sudoku puzzle on a regular basis. Today, bookstores, newsstands, websites and the like cannot keep up with the demand for Sudoku puzzles. Why all the excitement?

It all started back in 1979 when a "number place" puzzle appeared in the May issue of *Dell Pencil Puzzles and Crossword Games*. It required solvers to place numbers in cells within a grid. An editor at the magazine named Howard Garns is now credited as being its inventor. In 1984, another editor, this time for *Nikoli* magazines in Japan, came, by happenstance, across one of these puzzles. He loved it so much that he decided to put out an entire magazine devoted to it, which he called *Sudoku*. The term is an abbreviation of a Japanese expression that means "only single numbers allowed." Two years later, Sudoku became a craze across Japan.

In 1997, a retired judge from New Zealand named Wayne Gould saw a Sudoku puzzle magazine while working in Hong Kong. He too became fascinated by the puzzle and started making his own puzzles. His puzzles first appeared in *The Conway Daily Sun* in New Hampshire in 2004. Two months later, they appeared in *The Times* of London. By early 2005, Sudoku became a craze in Britain as well, quickly spreading throughout the globe from there.

Today, Sudoku is a permanent feature of newspapers alongside the ever-popular crossword puzzle. Why? In my view, it is the appeal of the pure logical thinking that is required to solve Sudoku, involving deduction and, sometimes, trial and error.

There's that word again—logic! That means left-hemisphere activity, as you know by now. Compared to the right hemisphere, this is what is known about the left hemisphere:

LEFT-HEMISPHERE FUNCTIONS	RIGHT-HEMISPHERE FUNCTIONS
language (in general)	intonation and music
literal meaning	metaphorical and emotional meaning
sequential relations	spatial relations
verbal memory	nonverbal memory
logical thinking	intuitive and spatial reasoning
abstracting and generalizing	concretizing and associating
analysis and linear thinking	synthesis and multiple thinking

Sudoku activates many of the functions on the left side of that chart. But it also activates a few on the right side as well, because you will have to make occasional guesses and try out a few possibilities as you go along.

Are you ready?

LATIN SQUARES

The idea behind Sudoku can be traced back to the Swiss mathematician Leonhard Euler (1707–1783), who invented a number game called "Latin squares" in 1783. His simple puzzle is the blueprint for Sudoku.

❁ Sample Puzzle

A Latin square is a square arrangement of digits placed in such a way that no digit appears twice in the same row or column. In the square at right, which is a four-by-four square, the first four digits—1, 2, 3, 4—each occur just once in each row and column. The second row and column have been highlighted for you.

The goal of the Latin square puzzle is to reconstruct its layout, since numbers will be missing from it. Note that a four-by-four square is filled with the first four digits, a five-

1	2	3	4
2	1	4	3
3	4	1	2
4	3	2	1

by-five with the first five digits and so on. That's all there is to it. The puzzles in this section are arranged in order of increasing difficulty, from very easy to relatively hard. ●

Let's start with five-by-five Latin squares. Insert the missing numbers in each square. Each number (1, 2, 3, 4, 5) occurs once in each row and column.

1.

5	4	3	2	
		1	5	2
3			4	5
2	5	4	1	3
1	2			4

2.

	4	5		2
3			5	
4			2	1
5	1	2	4	
	3			

The next two are also five-by-five squares. This time, however, there is a small twist to each puzzle. The cells of the two diagonals (highlighted for you) must also contain the five digits exactly once.

3.

5	2	1		4
3				5
4		3		
				3
2	3		4	1

4.

	3	5		4
5			1	3
4			5	2
	5	2		
2		1		

Now, try your hand at solving larger Latin squares—two six-by-six, two seven-by-seven and two nine-by-nine puzzles. A six-by-six square will have the first six digits in it distributed according to the usual rule (each digit must occur only once in each column and in each row); a seven-by-seven will have the first seven digits in it; and so on. Let's start with the two six-by-six puzzles.

5.

		4	3	2	1
5		1	6		
4	6		5		3
3	1			6	4
		6	1	3	5
1	2	3	4		

6.

		2	5		
		6	1		
4			2	3	5
3	5	4			2
2		5			4
		3	4	5	6

HINT

You might have to try a few numbers in a cell before determining which one belongs there. It is advisable to use a pencil so that you can erase any placement that doesn't work out. In addition, look at rows and columns simultaneously. This might give you a correct scanning of the placement possibilities.

Next, try solving two seven-by-seven puzzles. Things are getting a little harder, logically speaking.

7.

1	6	7	4			2
4			5	6	2	7
7			6	4	1	
6	5	4	7			1
2	7	1	3			4
		6	2	1	7	
5		2	1			6

8.

	2	5		4	7	
2		1			5	3
3	5		6	1	4	
4		2		3	1	7
		3	1			4
		4		7		5
7		6	4		2	

Finally, try these two nine-by-nine puzzles. They will hone your logic skills in preparation for Sudoku, since they will prepare you mentally to look systematically for specific kinds of number placement possibilities.

9.

8	4	5	3	1			7	6
2			6	8	5		3	4
1			7	4	9	8		2
6		3	4	9	1	7	2	5
	5	9	2			6	1	3
	2	1	5			4	8	
9			8	3	6		4	1
5			9	2	4	3	6	7
3	6	4	1	5	7	2		

10.

		4	1	7	6	5		3
3			2	9			4	1
2			3	4	5	8		
6		9	5	1	2	3		4
5	8	2			9	1		6
1	4	3			7		5	2
		5	7	2	4	6	1	8
	2	1	8	6		4		
4	6			5		2		

To grasp how Sudoku is solved, it is useful to start with a reduced version of the standard puzzle. This will allow you to warm up, logically speaking. You have already been practicing the basic idea behind it, by the way. Let's look at a four-by-four version.

✸ Sample Puzzle

The objective is to complete the grid logically by placing each of the first four digits (1, 2, 3, 4) in each row and each column within the entire (four-by-four) grid as well as inside each two-by-two box (marked out by thicker lines)—without repetition! That's the only rule there is in Sudoku. Notice that this puzzle is really nothing more than four two-by-two Latin squares combined.

Start by reasoning out the correct location of the digits 1 and 2 missing from the top right box. As you can see, you could also start by focusing on the bottom left box or even either of the second or third rows of the grid. You do not know in which order 1 and 2 will eventually work out, so try both.

A   **B**

Look at the third column of the grid in layout A. To complete that column, you will need to place the digits 2 and 4 in it. You cannot put the 2 in the third cell down, because a 2 already exists in the third row of the grid and repetition is not allowed. Look at what would happen if you did put the 2 there. As you can see in the diagram to the left, the 2 would be repeated in the third row (highlighted for you).

Putting the 4 there would also not work out, because there is a 4 already in that row (as you can see highlighted in the diagram to the right).

		1	2
		3	4
4	2	2	
		4	

		1	2
		3	4
4	2	4	
		2	

There is no way to complete the column. The only logical conclusion is that possibility A should be eliminated because it does not work. Possibility B is the only way to go. Let's reproduce it here:

B

		2	1
		3	4
4	2		

Look at the third column of the grid again. You must place 1 and 4 in that column, since 2 and 3 are already in it. You cannot put 4 in the third cell from the top because a repetition would result (shown in the diagram to the left below). The only possible placement is in the fourth cell of the third row, shown in the diagram to the right. This completes the third column.

		2	1
		3	4
4	2	4	
		1	

		2	1
		3	4
4	2	1	
		4	

This leaves only one number for the last cell of the third row down from the top—3— since the other numbers (4, 2 and 1) are already in the row. This is shown in the diagram to the left below.

This leaves 2 as the missing digit completing both the last column and the bottom box simultaneously (shown in the diagram to the right).

		2	1
		3	4
4	2	1	3
	4		

		2	1
		3	4
4	2	1	3
		4	2

So far, so good. There are no repetitions in the two completed boxes and no repetitions in the two completed columns and one row. Moving on to the top row, the digits 3 and 4 are missing from it. You cannot put 4 in the first cell, because this would produce a repetition with the 4 below in the first row (shown in the diagram to the left below). The only possibility is shown in the diagram to the right.

4	3	2	1
		3	4
4	2	1	3
		4	

3	4	2	1
		3	4
4	2	1	3
		4	2

In the second row down, the numbers 1 and 2 are missing. You cannot put the 2 in the second cell, because this would produce a repetition just below it (shown in the diagram to the left). The only possible placement of the two numbers is shown in the diagram to the right.

3	4	2	1
1	2	3	4
4	2	1	3
		4	2

3	4	2	1
2	1	3	4
4	2	1	3
		4	2

The rest is easy. The completed grid looks like this:

3	4	2	1
2	1	3	4
4	2	1	3
1	3	4	2

Try your hand at the following six four-by-four puzzles. They are arranged in order of increasing difficulty, although overall they are still easy to solve. They are designed to activate your logical skills in a straightforward fashion.

11.

1			4
	4	2	
	3	1	
2	1	4	3

12.

3			4
	1	2	
	3	4	
1			2

13.

1			
	4	3	
	2	1	
3			4

14.

			2
	1	4	
	2	3	
1			

15.

1			3
		4	
	1		
4		1	

16.

4			
	2	3	
	4	2	

Next, solve the following four six-by-six puzzles. This time you will have to place the first six digits (1, 2, 3, 4, 5, 6) in each box and in each row and column of the grid with no repetitions. The logic involved is getting harder, by the way.

17.

1	2				6
4		6	1	2	3
		1	2		5
	6	2	3		1
2	3	5		1	
6			5		2

18.

	1		5	6	
	5	6	2		
	3		6	4	5
6		5			
5	6				3
3			4	5	6

19.

6		1			3
		3	5		
		5	6		
2	1	6			5
5				3	4
1	3				6

20.

	6	1	5	2	
4	5			1	3
	2	3		4	5
5	1			3	
			4	6	
				5	2

STANDARD PUZZLES

In its standard form, a Sudoku puzzle is laid out as a nine-by-nine grid. The grid is further divided into nine three-by-three boxes. The objective is to place the numbers 1 through 9 in every row and column of the grid, as well as in every box, without repetition. In other words, you will need to use the same logic from the previous puzzles to cover a broader territory. The puzzles are arranged in order of increasing difficulty.

A FEW HINTS

- Look over the entire puzzle first, identifying a box, a row or a column where only one number will fit in a cell or else where only several numbers will fit in some order.
- Go back and forth among boxes, columns and rows until you spot a unique placement. Don't get stuck, literally, inside a box!
- When you think you know the number or numbers, pencil them in lightly. You might have to erase them later if you have made a mistake.

21.

	3		7	9		2	5	8
	7	9		8	2	6	1	
	8					9		7
7			4			8	9	1
		8	9	2	3		7	
9	6		8	1	7	3	2	
		7		3	9	1	8	2
8	9		2		1	7		3
	1	2		7	8	5	4	9

22.

		7	9	6	5		1	4
6		8	2			3		9
9		4	1			7		6
1		6	4		2	5	8	7
5		3		1			6	
7		2				1	4	3
8						2		1
2		9	3	5	1	4	7	8
	3	1	7	2		6		5

A FEW MORE HINTS

- Never guess, since this may lead to an incorrect placement.
- Sometimes, several possibilities exist for a specific cell. In such a case, set up several scenarios, as in the warm-up sample puzzle, eliminating the scenario that doesn't work out.
- For this reason, draw several layouts of the puzzle on worksheets, labeling them *Scenario A, Scenario B* and so on.
- You might have to follow a single number across rows and columns while you consider its placement in a box. This kind of crisscrossing analysis will often tell you that a certain number cannot be in a certain place and thus it must occur elsewhere.

23.

9	4	7	2	6	8	1	5	3
		5	4			7	6	9
	6	3	9	5	1		8	7
1	3	2					9	6
					8			1
7	8	9				3		
	9	1	5	2	6		4	8
		8	1			9		2
4	2		8	7	9		1	5

- There are now an infinitude of versions of this simple, yet challenging, puzzle. Most involve larger and larger layouts. But all are solved with the same logic.
- The number of possible Sudoku puzzles that can be made with the first nine digits is calculated to be 6,670,903,752,021,072,936,960! It would take a computer over 211 billion years to solve them all.
- There are now so many Sudoku competitions and tournaments throughout the world that it would take an entire book simply to list them.
- Perhaps the most comprehensive book on the history and many versions of Sudoku is *The Addict's Guide to Everything Sudoku*, by Fiorella Grossi (Fair Winds, 2007).
- The Alzheimer's Association in the United States has endorsed Sudoku as a preventive strategy against the dreaded disease. Their recommendation is based on published studies, such as a 2003 one in *The New England Journal of Medicine*, that strongly suggest that Sudoku may indeed help prevent dementia.
- If you want more Sudoku challenges, here are some online resources:

www.sudoku.com	www.brainfreezepuzzles.com
www.sudokusolver.com	www.sudoku-league.com
www.sudokudragon.com	www.indigopuzzles.com

24.

6			8		3	1	4	9
			7					6
4			1		6	8	7	5
2	3	5				6	1	8
	1	4	2	6	8			3
8	6	9			1	4	2	7
1	4	6	5	3	7			2
3		8	6					
	7	2	9	8	4		6	

25.

6		8	7		5		3	2
	7	3			9	1		8
2	9			1	8	4		6
	5	7			6		2	4
9	2				1	3	6	
	8		2	7		5	9	1
	6		1		3	7	4	
7		1					8	
		9	4		7	2	1	

26.

9		5		4	1	2		6
			2		5	3	1	
2		8	3		7		9	
5		6		7	8	9		4
	9				4			
1		7				6		2
3		2	9	8		7	4	1
6	7		4		3	8		
	8	9		1	2			

27.

9		2	4	7			8	6
5		1	3	6			2	4
	4	7	1	2	8	3	5	
2	1	5	9	4	7			
3	6			8	2			
8	7			3	1			
			8	1			4	5
		3	2	9			1	7
			7	5	4	2	6	3

28.

2	4					6	1	
		7	2				5	
9			1	4	5	3		
	5	1		2	4		3	9
6	3			7	9	5	4	1
								2
		3	4	9	6		7	
5					1	2	9	
1	6			5	2	4		

29.

			4	1	2	5		
	2	4			8	6	1	
	8	3		2				
	3	1		9	2	5		6
6	4			8	3			
	7					3		1
3	1		4	5		8		9
		7	8	1			3	
	6	8		3			7	5

30.

3			9	8		4		
2		4		6				
		8				1	5	6
6			1	5	4			
5	3	2		9	8	7		
4					2	8	6	
			2	1	5	3	9	
	2						7	1
1	5	3		7				2

The next four puzzles are variations on the same theme. They use the first nine letters in place of digits (A, B, C, D, E, F, G, H, I). Apparently, this makes them more difficult, although it is not clear why this is so—perhaps the brain handles numbers more easily than letters.

The same rules apply; that is, you must place each of the nine letters in each row, column and box with no repetitions. They are arranged in order of increasing difficulty, from moderately easy to quite difficult. You will really be sharpening your basic logic skills with these.

31.

E	A		I		G	C		F
G	H	D	F		C	A	B	I
	F		H	A	B	E	G	D
A		C	B	I	F	H	E	
			G	C			F	A
I			A	H			C	B
D	E	G		F		B	I	H
B			D	G	I	F		E
F				B	H	G	D	C

32.

	I	B		H	C		G	E
H		G	E		I	F	A	B
E	F	D	G	B		H		
	H	E		C	B		F	D
F	D		H	I		E	B	
	A	H		G	E		D	F
G	E	I		F	D	A	C	
	B	F	C	A	H	I	E	

33.

		A	B			C		G
		H	A	I	C		B	
C	B	F			G	D		A
	C		G	B		H	A	D
		D			A		C	B
B	A	G	C	D		F		
			D	C	B	A		E
A		B		G			D	C
E	D	C		A		B		

HINT

If you are having difficulty solving this version of Sudoku, convert the letters into numbers to create a standard layout of the puzzle. For example, $A = 1$, $B = 2$, $C = 3$, $D = 4$, $E = 5$, $F = 6$, $G = 7$, $H = 8$ and $I = 9$. When you have worked out the solution, do the reverse by replacing the numbers with the letters. After that, check your answer.

34.

E	D	I	C			B	F	
A		B	F	E	D		G	I
F	H		A				C	
	I	F		C				
			B	G			D	F
D		E					H	B
			G	I	C		B	D
I	F			D	B	G		H
	B			A		E		

PLACEMENT ADDITION PUZZLES

Number placement has given reign to the construction of many kinds of logic puzzles. One type has characteristics of both Latin and magic squares (which are coming up in the next chapter). These puzzles can be called "placement addition puzzles."

To solve this type of puzzle, fill in each cell in each row and column with a number from 1 to 9. There are only two rules. The numbers in a row must add up to the total shown in the last cell to the right of the row (marked out clearly for you). And the numbers in a column must add up to the total shown in the last cell at the bottom of the column (also marked out clearly for you).

Unlike other placement puzzles, any of the nine numbers can be used more than once, and not all nine numbers will be used in any row or column or even in the puzzle as a whole. You'll get the knack of what to do as you go along.

These puzzles require you to use the same kind of logic as other number placement puzzles. In addition, they force you to exercise your knowledge of arithmetic. In other words, they will give the logic areas of your brain a real workout.

As always, the puzzles are given to you in order of increasing difficulty. The first two are really easy and will help you get the hang of how to solve this type of puzzle.

35.

4		2		14
	2			10
5	6	3		22
	2		2	6
13	11	7	21	

36.

			2	5
3	9			25
5			2	9
2		8		12
11	12	16	12	

37.

2		5		16
1			5	24
	5	2		16
	6		2	18
20	23	17	14	

38.

	9		8	34
6	6			26
5		5		18
			2	5
21	21	19	22	

		5	**21**
	8		**25**
7		8	**18**
			4
22	**19**	**23**	**4**

4			4	**16**
	7	4		**19**
	2			**8**
		4	5	**11**
13	**14**	**16**	**11**	

	6	3		**11**
9			2	**13**
8			3	**19**
	4	1		**16**
25	**16**	**8**	**10**	

	5	4		**14**
		8	9	**34**
1			2	**6**
7	6			**19**
21	**20**	**19**	**13**	

KILLER PLACEMENT PUZZLES

Now your brain is going to get an even more energetic workout. The remaining puzzles are called killer placement puzzles. You will soon understand why.

In these puzzles, the highlighted number at the end of a row or a column will be either the sum of the numbers in that row or column or else their product (the numbers multiplied together). But the instructions will not tell you which is which.

The puzzles will start off relatively easy. In the first two puzzles, either all the columns or the rows are products or they are all sums and vice versa. That simplifies matters a little.

43.

2	2			4
3		3		54
	7		2	28
5			5	50
11	14	7	10	

44.

2		3		7
	5			14
	2		2	6
			6	17
8	80	9	48	

For the rest of the puzzles, the figure at the end of a column or a row might be a product or it might be a sum, in no particular pattern. You will have to figure out which is which. Otherwise, the same rules apply.

To increase the difficulty level even more so, an extra row and column have been added to puzzles 45–48 below. And in puzzles 49 and 50, there are six rows and columns.

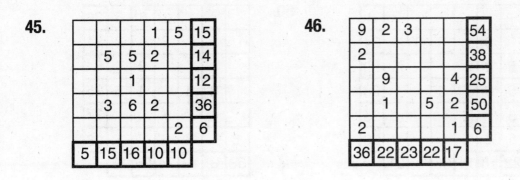

45.

			1	5	15
	5	5	2		14
		1			12
	3	6	2		36
			2		6
5	15	16	10	10	

46.

9	2	3			54
2					38
		9		4	25
	1		5	2	50
2				1	6
36	22	23	22	17	

HINTS

Keep in mind that there is no pattern. Only one column might be a product-producing one (that is, whose numbers are multiplied together—or two or three or four). On the other hand, all four columns and a few rows as well might be product-producing ones. You will simply have to put your logic cap on tightly.

You might need to make one or two hypotheses about what number(s) to place in a particular cell or cells. Remember to use a pencil so that you can erase wrong inferences.

Another technique is to make yourself several copies of the puzzle, inserting possibilities in each one simultaneously and discarding the ones that do not work out. In this way, you will get a solution by the process of elimination, which is a very good brain exercise in and of itself.

47.

	9	1		1	**15**
	2	2		3	**48**
	8				**20**
2			2		**24**
3				3	**9**
11	**21**	**20**	**9**	**81**	

48.

4	1		2		**32**
4	8		3		**19**
	8	7		2	**19**
		7	5		**23**
4		7		1	**21**
64	**33**	**23**	**30**	**48**	

49.

				2		**2**
	6		9	3	4	**24**
5	2		1		5	**50**
5	6		9			**23**
5		5				**25**
5	2	5	9		8	**30**
22	**18**	**14**	**30**	**8**	**21**	

50.

			2	5	6	**26**
			2	4	2	**21**
				2		**54**
	3	3		4	5	**25**
						27
8		3	6		1	**28**
53	**3**	**18**	**24**	**25**	**16**	

7
BRAINTEASERS

*Mathematics alone make us feel the
limits of our intelligence.*
SIMONE WEIL

THE WORD *BRAINTEASER* IS AN APPROPRIATE ONE to describe the puzzles in this chapter, since they are all designed to tease the brain. That is, these puzzles annoy your brain so that the mathematical juices within can start flowing, especially if they have been stagnant for a while.

Math! For many of us that word brings with it memories of tedious addition, subtraction, multiplication and division of numbers. Where's the pleasure in doing that, one may ask. As Lord Byron once said, "I know that two and two make four and should be glad to prove it too if I could—though I must say if by any sort of process I could convert two and two into five it would give me much greater pleasure."

Enter the brainteaser, to add spice and interest to basic math, clothing it in an interesting guise. In fact, the brainteaser genre has actually brought about many discoveries in math itself. As Edward Kasner and James Newman note in their classic 1940 book, *Mathematics and the Imagination,* "the theory of equations, of probability, the infinitesimal calculus, the theory of point sets, of topology, all have grown out of problems first expressed in puzzle form."

In this chapter, you will come across some of the more interesting brainteaser genres.

These require only the ability to add, subtract, multiply, divide and do a few other basic operations. You will, however, have to use both your logical and lateral thinking skills as you solve magic squares, cryptarithms, alphametics and other numerical conundrums. What are those? You will soon find out, if you do not know already, but the puzzles in this chapter will give your brain—especially the left hemisphere—a very good workout.

MAGIC SQUARES

A magic square is a square that contains numbers arranged in rows and columns in such a way that the sum of the numbers in each row, column and diagonal is the same. That sum is called a magic sum or a magic constant.

You will get to know more about these puzzles as you go about solving them. Let's get started. As usual, the puzzles will be easy at first, getting harder and harder as you progress.

1. Let's start with a three-by-three square. Insert the first nine numbers (1, 2, 3, 4, 5, 6, 7, 8, 9) in its nine cells so that the numbers in each of its three rows, three columns and two diagonals add up to the same sum. You will be given a few number clues. Incidentally, what is that magic sum?

8		
	5	
		9

2. This is another version of a three-by-three magic square.

4		
		6

3. Here is yet another version of this square for you to construct.

8	3	

LO SHU

The square you solved in puzzle 3 is the original one, discovered in China over four thousand years ago and called *Lo Shu*. The Chinese ascribed mystical properties to Lo Shu. To this day, it is thought to provide protection against the evil eye when placed over the entrance to a dwelling or room. Fortune-tellers use it to cast fortunes. Amulets and talismans are commonly designed with Lo Shu inscribed on them.

4. Let's play a few variations on the same theme. Arrange the first nine even numbers (2, 4, 6, 8, 10, 12, 14, 16, 18) into a three-by-three magic square. What is the magic constant of the square?

5. Try your hand at arranging the first nine odd numbers (1, 3, 5, 7, 9, 11, 13, 15, 17) into a three-by-three magic square. What is the magic constant of the square?

6. This time, arrange the following nine consecutive numbers—8, 9, 10, 11, 12, 13, 14, 15, 16— into a three-by-three magic square. What is the magic constant of the square?

DO MAGIC SQUARES HAVE MAGICAL PROPERTIES?

Lo Shu spread from China to other parts of the world in the second century. Around 1300, the Greek mathematician Emanuel Moschopoulos introduced it to Europe. Like the Chinese, medieval astrologers perceived occult properties in these puzzles, using them to cast horoscopes.

They also saw them as concealing coded cosmic messages. The eminent astrologer Heinrich Cornelius Agrippa (1486–1535), for example, believed that a magic square of one cell (a square containing the single digit 1) represented the eternal perfection of God. Agrippa also took the fact that a two-by-two magic square cannot be constructed to be proof of the imperfection of the four elements: air, earth, fire and water.

7. The following puzzle was created by Henry E. Dudeney, whose name you have encountered several times already. Arrange the following nine numbers into a three-by-three magic square: 1, 7, 13, 31, 37, 43, 61, 67, 73. The magic constant of the square is 111.

8. The following puzzle is from another great puzzlist, Lewis Carroll, who used the postal values of his day to challenge magic square enthusiasts. In Victorian times, postage values were expressed in half units. Arrange the following postage stamps into a three-by-three magic square: 1d, 1½d, 2d, 2½d, 3d, 3½d, 4d, 4½d, 5d. What is the magic constant of the square?

	3d	

9. Let's move on to four-by-four magic squares. Insert the first sixteen digits (1, 2, 3, 4, . . . 16) in the sixteen cells so that the numbers in each of its four rows, four columns and two diagonals add up to the same sum. Some number clues are provided for you. What's the magic constant?

16			13
5			
			12
4			

ALBRECHT DÜRER

There are 880 possible solutions to a four-by-four magic square. The square you just solved was constructed by the great German painter Albrecht Dürer (1471–1528), which he included in his famous 1514 engraving *Melancholia*.

This magic square has amazing properties. For example, the magic constant of 34 appears not only as the sum of the rows, the columns and the diagonals, but in the following as well:

- in the sum of the digits in the four corners (16 + 13 + 4 + 1 = 34)
- in the sum of the four digits in the center (10 + 11 + 6 + 7 = 34)
- in the sum of the digits 15 and 14 in the bottom row and the digits 3 and 2 facing them in the top row (15 + 14 + 3 + 2 = 34)
- in the sum of the digits 12 and 8 in the right-hand column and 9 and 5 facing them in the left-hand column (12 + 8 + 9 + 5 = 34)

Can you spot any more instances?

10. For your last puzzle in this genre, construct a four-by-four magic square with magic constant 102. This is a difficult puzzle. Note that all the numbers used, except 1, are prime: 1, 3, 5, 7, 11, 13, 17, 19, 23, 29, 31, 37, 41, 47, 53, 71.

	71		
53			
			31
		19	

NUMBER PATTERNS

Look at the following computations and see if you detect any pattern.

2 x 9 = 18	and	1 + 8 = 9
3 x 9 = 27	and	2 + 7 = 9
4 x 9 = 36	and	3 + 6 = 9
5 x 9 = 45	and	4 + 5 = 9
. . .		
12 x 9 = 108	and	1 + 0 + 8 = 9
123 x 9 = 1,107	and	1 + 1 + 0 + 7 = 9
1,245 x 9 = 11,205	and	1 + 1 + 2 + 0 + 5 = 9
12,459 x 9 = 112,131	and	1 + 1 + 2 + 1 + 3 + 1 = 9

The digits of any multiple of nine, when added together, produce nine (or a multiple of nine). Patterns such as this abound throughout the numbers. In a fundamental sense, mathematics is the science of patterns.

As it turns out, numbers seem to be the "language of the universe," as the founder of mathematics, Pythagoras, claimed. No wonder, then, that early mathematics was thought to be a magical code revealing the secrets of the universe. Some of that sense of mystery is built into the next set of puzzles. As in previous chapters, the solution to this kind of puzzle tends to produce within us the "aha" effect—a simultaneous feeling of satisfaction and wonderment.

For each sequence, determine the next number in the sequence.

11. 1, 4, 7, 10, 13, 16, . . .

12. 4, 3, 5, 4, 6, 5, 7, . . .

13. 2, 4, 8, 16, 32, 64, . . .

14. 2, 3, 5, 7, 11, 13, 17, 19, . . .
(Be careful on this one!)

15. 1, 1, 2, 3, 5, 8, 13, 21, 34, . . .

16. 1, 1, 2, 4, 7, 13, 24, . . .

17. 3, 9, 27, 81, 243, 729, . . .

18. 16,807; 2,401; 343; 49; . . .

THE FIBONACCI SEQUENCE

The sequence in puzzle 15 is probably the most famous one in human history. It is known as the Fibonacci Sequence, after Leonardo Fibonacci (c. 1170–1240), the Italian mathematician who helped introduce Hindu-Arabic numerals (0, 1, 2, 3, 4, 5, 6, 7, 8, 9) into Western Europe, where the Roman numeral system was being used at the time. The sequence is found as part of a puzzle he composed in his 1202 book titled the *Liber Abaci* (Book of the Abacus).

The number of times the sequence crops up in nature and in human affairs is mind-boggling. Here's just one example. Daisies tend to have 21, 34, 55 or 89 petals (the eighth, ninth, tenth and eleventh numbers in the sequence); trilliums, wild roses, bloodroots, columbines, lilies and irises also have petals in consecutive Fibonacci numbers.

Fibonacci numbers also appear in the description of the reproduction of a population of bees. Basically, if one knows how to look, Fibonacci numbers can be found in plants, poems, symphonies, art forms, computers, the solar system and the stock market. Myriads of books and articles have been written on this topic.

You can read more about this fascinating sequence by going online at www.answers.com/topic/fibonacci-number.

19. 1, 4, 9, 16, 25, 36, . . .

20. 3, 2, 4, 5, 8, 12, 19, 30, . . .

21. 1, 100, 2, 99, 3, 98, 4, 97, 5, . . .

22. 2, 5, 4, 25, 8, 125, 16, 625, . . .

23. 1, 3, 2, 5, 7, 4, 9, 11, 6, 13, 15, . . .

24. 123, 321, 467, 764, 892, 298, 453, . . .

25. 4, 2, 2, 6, 3, 3, 8, 5, 3, 10, 7, 3, 12, 7, . . .

26. 12, 3, 24, 6, 35, 8, 49, 13, 58, 13, 62, . . .

27. 21, 1, 42, 2, 53, 2, 94, 5, 98, . . .

GOLDBACH'S CONJECTURE

The sequence in puzzle 25 is a very famous one in mathematics. Notice in the answer that the sequence consists of even integers, greater than two, that are rewritten as a sum of two primes. It would seem that every even number can be rewritten in this way—as the sum of two primes. This discovery was made by the mathematician Christian Goldbach (1690–1764), who pointed it out in a letter to Leonhard Euler in 1742.

No exception is known to Goldbach's conjecture, as it has been known ever since, but no valid proof of it yet exists.

In his enjoyable novel, *Uncle Petros and Goldbach's Conjecture* (2000), the Greek writer Apostolos Doxiadis argues that the conjecture is one of those revelations provided occasionally by God to mystify human ingenuity, even if it is doubtful that, should an explanation for the conjecture ever be revealed, it would change the world in any way. But then again, it might!

CRYPTARITHMS

The term *cryptarithm* was originally coined by a pseudonymous Maurice Vatriquant in the May 1931 issue of the Belgian magazine *Sphinx*. A cryptarithm is a puzzle in which some or all of the digits in an addition, subtraction, division or multiplication layout have been deleted. You are asked to reconstruct the layout by deducing numerical values on the basis of the mathematical relationships indicated by the various arrangements and locations of the given numbers. Cryptarithms are, in effect, the arithmetical counterparts of cryptograms.

28. As always, let's start off with an easy puzzle. Below is an addition problem with some of its numbers missing for you to reconstruct.

```
      *  2
  +   5  *
  ─────────
   *  0  4
```

29. Here's another addition puzzle. This one is a bit harder to reconstruct.

```
      8  *  2  *
  +   *  2  0  *
  ────────────────
   *  8  0  2  2
```

30. Now try your hand at a subtraction cryptarithm.

```
   *  5  *
  -     *  9
  ──────────
      2  9  9
```

31. This cryptarithm is also a subtraction problem.

```
    *  3  *
 -  1  *  0
 ─────────
       4  4
```

32. Let's move on to a multiplication cryptarithm.

```
       *  8
 x        *
 ─────────
    *  2  4
```

33. Here's another multiplication cryptarithm.

```
    9  *  *
 x        9
 ─────────
 *  *  9  1
```

34. Here's one more multiplication cryptarithm where only the fives have been preserved.

```
       5  *  *
 x        *  5
 ───────────
    *  5  5  5
    5  *  *
 ───────────
    *  *  *  5
```

In the remaining cryptarithms, you are presented with an equation in which the operation signs (+, −, ×, ÷) are missing. Put them in correctly.

35.　45 * 98 * 3 = 140

36.　12 * 3 * 4 = 9

37.　98 * 2 * 7 * 2 = 14

38.　2 * 34 * 12 * 1 = 48

39.　15 * 21 * 3 * 4 = 3

40.　12 * 9 * 5 * 2 * 8 = 4

ALPHAMETICS

In 1924, Henry Dudeney came up with a different genre of cryptarithm puzzle in which he replaced all the numbers in an addition, subtraction, multiplication or division layout with letters, making actual words. In 1955, the American puzzlist J. A. H. Hunter referred to this genre as an *alphametic* (short for *alphabet arithmetic*). Alphametics are brainteasers that will tax, rather than just tease, your arithmetical brain. If they fascinate you, you can get your fill of them at www.alphametics.com.

41. *No to ten.* Each letter of this phrase stands for a specific digit. Replace the letters with the digits they stand for to reconstruct the addition below and, thus, decipher what no + to = ten means.

```
    n o
+   t o
───────
  t e n
```

42. *Pop, tot, mama.* This alphametic is a bit tougher.

```
    p o p
+   t o t
─────────
  m a m a
```

43. *Aha!* This next one involves multiplication.

```
      a h a
x       h a
───────────
      t a t
    a h a
───────────
    a s t t
```

In the last line, ASTT is an acronym for *alphametics simply take time.* This has nothing to do with solving the puzzle; it's just an interesting side note.

44. Here's Dudeney's original puzzle.

```
    s e n d
+   m o r e
───────────
  m o n e y
```

The last set of classic brainteasers in this chapter is a mixed lot.

45. There are between fifty and sixty ties in a drawer. If you count them three at a time, you will find that there are two left over. If you count them five at a time, you will find that there are four left over. How many ties are there in the drawer?

46. If a pencil and eraser together cost 55 cents, and the pencil costs 50 cents more than the eraser costs, what does the eraser cost?

47. Yesterday, I bought an antique clock, which strikes the number of hours every hour. At eight o'clock, it needs seven seconds to make eight strikes. For how many seconds each day does the clock strike?

48. Gina works every second day at a convenience store. Alexander also works there, but every third day. The store stays open seven days a week, from Monday through Sunday. This week, Gina started work on Tuesday, June 1, and Alexander on Wednesday, June 2. On what date will the two work together next?

49. This one is in the same genre as puzzle 48. Jack works every third day at a nearby store. Sarah also works there, but only on Saturdays. The store stays open seven days a week, from Monday through Sunday. This week, Jack worked on Monday, October 1. On what date will the two work together next?

50. My sister has two dimes. If four-fifths of what my sister has equals eight-ninths of what I have, how much money do I have?

8
WORD PLAY

One forgets words as one forgets names. One's vocabulary
needs constant fertilizing or it will die.
EVELYN WAUGH

AS MENTIONED IN THE INTRODUCTION TO THIS BOOK, the oldest puzzle known is the Riddle of the Sphinx. It is a perfect example of how riddles tell a fascinating anecdotal side story about human existence. From childhood, we are instinctively drawn to riddles, clearly enjoying both the challenge they pose and the mischievous language with which they have been composed. And yet, in all likelihood, no one has ever discussed with us what a riddle is or how to seek an answer to the conundrum it poses. Is there something more to riddles than just verbal fun?

Like the Riddle of the Sphinx, the puzzles in this chapter all involve some form of word play. They are designed to activate the language centers of your brain, especially language memory centers. In the late 1800s, scientists observed that damage to particular parts of the brain caused the same language disabilities in most patients. They found that damage to the left frontal lobe in Broca's area destroyed the ability to enunciate. Damage to the left temporal lobe in Wernicke's area caused difficulty in comprehending and remembering language.

Modern imaging technologies, such as PET and fMRI, have enabled neuroscientists to observe the brain directly while people speak, listen, read and think. The results have shown that language processing is extremely complex, unlike what the nineteenth- and twentieth-century neuroscientists thought (with few exceptions). Language areas are spread widely through the brain, and different types of language tasks activate these areas in many sequences and patterns. Thus, puzzles involving word play should, arguably, activate all those areas—at least that's what the research appears to suggest.

Above all else, word play stimulates memory and the imaginative centers in the right hemisphere (where figurative language, for example, is processed), since you will have to dig deeply into your memory banks to flesh out the patterns that produce the required solutions.

RIDDLES

Those who were incapable of solving the Riddle of the Sphinx paid for their ineptitude with their lives. The Sphinx, as legend would have it, devoured anyone daring to enter the city of Thebes, which she guarded night and day, who could not answer her riddle.

Oedipus did answer her riddle. Although he was not killed by the Sphinx, we know what happened to him nonetheless. And all this over a riddle!

Now it's your turn to solve riddles. As always, these will start off easy. A hint is provided for the first five puzzles in the form of the first letter of the required word.

1. It flies, yet it has no wings.
It can be long and short, yet it is not a measuring stick.
It can be put into a capsule, but it is not a medicine.
What is it?
(Hint: The first letter is *t*.)

2. What is it that everyone uses more than you do,
yet it belongs to you?
(Hint: The first letter is *n*.)

3. Its colors are red, blue, purple and green.
You can easily see that.
But you can't touch it or even reach it.
What is it?
(Hint: The first letter is *r*.)

RIDDLES IN MYTH AND LEGEND

Samson's life ended in calamity over a riddle he posed to the Philistines, as those who are familiar with the Bible story can attest.

Also in the Old Testament, Josephus writes that Hiram (the king of Tyre) and Solomon waged a riddle contest against each other.

The ancient Greek priests and priestesses, known as oracles, were wont to express their more ominous prophecies in the form of riddles.

Riddles also appear in narratives—in the fairy tales of the Brothers Grimm, in the Mother Goose nursery rhymes, and in J. R. R. Tolkein's *The Lord of the Rings,* among many others. And let's not forget pop culture, where the Riddler, of Batman comic fame, is a well-known villain who always has a riddle handy.

4. It can be bitter or sweet, but it is neither food nor drink.
It can blossom and grow, but it is not a plant.
What is it?
(Hint: The first letter is *l.*)

5. It can be put on scales, but it is not a substance.
It is blind, but it is not a human being.
What is it?
(Hint: The first letter is *j.*)

6. It can be Promethean.
It can be infernal.
And, of course, it can be eternal.
What is it?

7. It can be golden, but it is not a metal.
It can be of one's eye, but it is not a human organ.
Some would even say it is forbidden.
What is it?

8. You can raise it, though it has no weight.
People with money might embody it.
As can some jobs.
What is it?

9. It can be made of honey.
Its color can be of silver.
When it's full, strange things happen.

10. You can wear it and take it off, but it is neither clothes nor shoes.
What is it?

ANAGRAMS

An anagram is a word or phrase formed from another by transposing or rearranging the letters. For example, *north* becomes *thorn*.

Some of the anagrams you will be working with in this section are quite famous, having tickled people's fancy (or else given them headaches) for a long time. They are now part of an "anagram encyclopedia," as it may be called. Attribution for an anagram (if known and when appropriate) is shown at the end of each one.

✸ Word-to-Word Anagrams

Let's start with the basic type of anagram puzzle in which the letters of a given word are rearranged to produce one or more new words. For example, the word *evil* can be rewritten as *veil* or *live*.

If more than one word can be made, the number is given in parentheses following. For example, *pots* in number 11 will yield four words (as far as I can tell). However, you might be able to find more anagrams for each given word.

11. Ⓐ care (2)

Ⓑ trace

Ⓒ pots (4)

Ⓓ tips (2)

Ⓔ Elvis (2)

12. Ⓐ persist

Ⓑ riptides

Ⓒ listen (2)

Ⓓ admirer

Ⓔ stone (3)

> **LANGUAGE ON VACATION!**
>
> If you want more anagram fun, go online at http://wordsmith.org/anagram. There you can input any word or phrase, including your name, and you will get it anagrammatized automatically. You are also bound to come across a number of the anagrams you have solved here. Anagrams, it would seem, are everywhere!

✳ Word-to-Phrase/Phrase-to-Word Anagrams

In the next set of anagrams, the idea is to produce either: (1) a single phrase (or sentence) by anagrammatizing a given word: for example, *astronomer* will yield, rather appropriately, *moon starer;* or (2) a single word by anagrammatizing a given phrase: for example, the letters in the phrase *Is pity love?* can be rearranged to form the single word *Positively!* By the way, you might have to capitalize some letters or lowercase others, as well as add or delete an apostrophe or add or delete spaces.

The difficulty level, as you can see, is going up. Again, you will find classic puzzles in the mix. And, as before, you might be able to come up with other answers than the ones given, though those other answers must make sense.

13. phrase anagrams

Ⓐ spiderman (two-word phrase)

Ⓑ helicopters (two-word phrase)

Ⓒ dormitory (two-word phrase)

Ⓓ schoolmaster (two-word phrase)

Ⓔ gladiator (three-word phrase)

14. phrase anagrams

    Ⓐ telegraph (two-word phrase)

    Ⓑ funeral (two-word phrase)

    Ⓒ Presbyterian (three-word phrase)

    Ⓓ earnestness (three-word phrase)

    Ⓔ Christianity (four-word phrase) *(Henry B. Wheatley)*

15. single-word anagrams

    Ⓐ voices rant on

    Ⓑ life's aim

    Ⓒ flutter by

    Ⓓ swear oft

    Ⓔ no more stars

✸ Phrase-to-Phrase Anagrams

From the letters of each given phrase, can you form another phrase? For example, the letters of the phrase *the golden days,* when properly rearranged, will yield the sentence *They gladden so!* Again, you might have to add or delete an apostrophe or space here and there, as well as capitalize a letter, to get the solution.

FAMOUS ANAGRAMS

Are anagrams prophetic messages? Two by the great British writer and puzzlist Lewis Carroll seem to lend some credence to this. One is on the name of the British humanitarian Florence Nightingale (1820–1910), which provides her with a fitting eulogy, and the other is on the name of the British political agitator William Ewart Gladstone (1809–1898), which brings out Gladstone's firebrand personality:

Florence Nightingale   =   Flit on, cheering angel!

William Ewart Gladstone   =   Wild agitator! Means well!

But perhaps the most famous anagram, which was constructed retrospectively to explain a person's fate in life, was the one of Mary, Queen of Scots (1542–1587), who died by execution. She was posthumously memorialized with the Latin expression *Trusavi regnis morte amara cada* ("Thrust by force from my kingdom I fall by a foul death"), which, incredibly, is an anagram of *Maria Steuarda Scotarum Regina* ("Mary Stewart, Queen of Scots")!

You will find classic puzzles in this set (old and current) and, again, you might be able to find other solutions than the ones given.

16. Ⓐ the eyes

    Ⓑ the summer vacation

    Ⓒ Statue of Liberty

    Ⓓ eleven plus two

    Ⓔ old masters

17. Ⓐ vacation times

    Ⓑ the detectives

    Ⓒ a gentleman

    Ⓓ debit card *(Mike Morton)*

    Ⓔ It's a wonderful life!

This time you are given the names of famous people. By anagrammatizing the letters of their names, you will get an interesting word or phrase about them. Again, you might have to make punctuation, spacing and capitalization alterations. And as before, some of these are classics, while others are making the rounds as I write.

18. Ⓐ Tom Cruise

    Ⓑ Alec Guinness *(Dick Cavett)*

    Ⓒ Martin Scorsese

    Ⓓ George Bush *(Mike Morton)*

    Ⓔ Ronald Reagan

19. Ⓐ David Letterman

    Ⓑ Madonna

    Ⓒ Tonya Harding *(Tim DeLaney)*

    Ⓓ Henry Wadsworth Longfellow

    Ⓔ England's Queen Victoria

ANAGRAMS IN HISTORY

Anagram traditions based on prophecy are found throughout ancient cultures. Legend has it that even Alexander the Great (356–323 BCE) believed in their prophetic power. During the siege of the city of Tyre, Alexander was particularly troubled by a dream he had in which a satyr appeared to him. The next morning, he summoned his soothsayers to interpret the dream. They pointed out to Alexander that the word *satyr* itself contained the answer, because in Greek, "satyr" is an anagram of "Tyre is thine." Reassured, Alexander went on to conquer the city on the subsequent day.

One of the most famous anagrams of all time was devised in the Middle Ages. Its unknown author contrived it as a Latin dialogue between Pilate and Jesus. Jesus' answer to Pilate's question "What is truth?" is phrased as an ingenious anagram of the letters of that very question:

Pilate: *Quid est veritas?* ("What is truth?")

Jesus: *Est vir qui adest.* ("It is the man before you.")

✸ Antigrams

For your last puzzle set in this section, try your hand at antigrams. As its name implies, an antigram is the opposite of an anagram. That is, by rearranging the letters of a word or phrase, you will get a word or phrase that means the opposite. For example, the antigram of *evangelists* is *evil's agents*. (By the way, the creator of that antigram was Evertt Ewing in 1927.)

As with anagrams, you might have to make capitalization, spacing and punctuation changes.

20. Ⓐ united
Ⓑ ill fed
Ⓒ more tiny
Ⓓ restful
Ⓔ anarchists *(W. L. Sacrey)*

ZIGGURATS

A ziggurat is an ancient pyramid-shaped tower with a square base. The puzzle version of this shape goes like this. You start off at the top with a four-letter word to be guessed according to the definition that is given to you. Then you work downward, adding the indicated letter to the higher-up word through anagrammatization.

✸ A Sample Ziggurat

Here's an example of a four-level ziggurat (the highest level we will challenge you with in this section).

Peel or cut back
Type of curtain (+*D*)
Knock, past participle (+*P*)
Ensnared (+*T*)

The answer to the top clue is *pare*. You have to get this right to start off. Let's put it in our ziggurat:

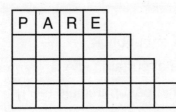

Peel or cut back

Type of curtain (+*D*)

Knock, past participle (+*P*)

Ensnared (+*T*)

The (+ *d*) in the second clue down tells us that by adding the letter *d* to the previous four-letter word (*pare*) and rearranging the resulting five letters, we will get a type of curtain. The answer? *Drape*.

P	A	R	E		
D	R	A	P	E	

Peel or cut back

Type of curtain (+*D*)

Knock, past participle (+*P*)

Ensnared (+*T*)

The third clue down tells us that by adding a *p* to the previous word (*drape*) and rearranging the resulting six letters, we will get the past participle of a verb meaning "to knock." The answer is *rapped* (the past participle of *rap*), which means "knocked."

P	A	R	E		
D	R	A	P	E	
R	A	P	P	E	D

Peel or cut back

Type of curtain (+*D*)

Knock, past participle (+*P*)

Ensnared (+*T*)

Finally, the last clue down tells us that by adding a *t* to the previous word *(rapped)* and rearranging the resulting seven letters, we will get a word meaning "ensnared." The answer is *trapped*. ⬡

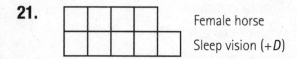

P	A	R	E			

Peel or cut back

| D | R | A | P | E |

Type of curtain (+*D*)

| R | A | P | P | E | D |

Knock, past participle (+*P*)

| T | R | A | P | P | E | D |

Ensnared (+*T*)

You will start off with a few two-level ziggurats, followed by several three-level ones and then four-level ones.

21.

Female horse
Sleep vision (+*D*)

22.

Paid regularly by a tenant
Fashion or mode (+*D*)

23.

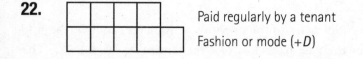

Running contest
A hoist (+*N*)

24.

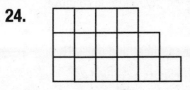

Do not put this before the horse, as the expression goes

A footprint or physical sign left behind (+*E*)

What someone does when he or she responds impulsively (+*S*)

25.

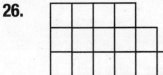

Type of shawl

Region beyond Earth's atmosphere (+*S*)

Locations (+*L*)

26.

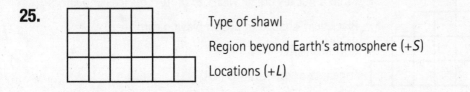

We're always trying to bring things about by making these meet

Computer geeks or whizzes (+*R*)

Fads (+*T*)

27.

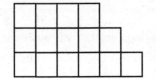

When you have four of these, no one can beat you at poker

Stop (+*E*)

A fold, or a place where a hockey goaltender stays (+*R*)

28.

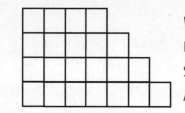

What you put your house up for, if you intend to move

Rent, let out (+E)

Substance that fastens or closes something up (+R)

A crowd . . . is someone who delights a crowd (+P)

29.

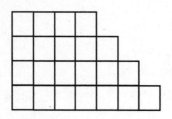

What a hockey goalie wears to protect his legs and knees

Black, leaf-shaped figure on playing cards (+E)

Curtains (+R)

Pageants or processions (+A)

30.

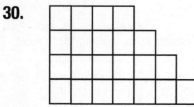

Painful, tender

Holes (+P)

Small (one-celled) bodies produced by algae, fungi, etc. (+S)

What someone does when he or she is tired (+E)

WORD SQUARES

A word square is a type of Latin square (remember those in Chapter 6?) with words instead of numbers. Word squares look simpler than they really are, so don't be fooled; they will still give your brain a good workout.

⊛ Sample Word Square

Complete this simple word square by inserting the seven given letters to the right into the grid, one per cell, to create the same words reading across and down. No proper names are allowed.

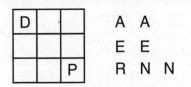

D must be followed by one of the given vowels, otherwise no real word would result. Either *A* or *E* could work, as there are two of each. Let's try the *As*, inserting them in both cells.

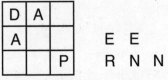

Of the remaining letters available to be inserted, the only one that would create a word is *N*:

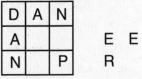

A *dan* is either a black belt level in the martial arts or a small buoy. However, there is no way to insert the remaining letters to create legitimate words. We can conclude, therefore, that the letter should be *E* instead. Let's insert both *Es* and the *Ns* in their appropriate cells.

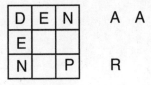

The only way to insert the remaining letters is:

D	E	N
E	R	A
N	A	P

The crisscrossing words in the square are *den*, *era* and *nap*. ⊛

Now it's your turn. You will start off with a couple of three-by-three grids, then several four-by-four grids and a final and very difficult five-by-five grid.

31.

O	N	

W W W T
O
E E

PALINDROMES

One of the words in puzzle 31 is a *palindrome;* that is, it can be read from left to right or backward, from right to left. Other examples of single-word palindromes include *civic, mom, dad, madam, level* and *deed.* Word palindromes are relatively rare in English. Sentence palindromes are even rarer. Here are several famous ones:

Madam, I'm Adam.

A man, a plan, a canal—Panama.

Niagara, O roar again.

Too far Edna, we wander afoot.

Palindromes require making adjustments to punctuation, spacing and capitalization. Can you think up any?

As difficult as palindrome sentences are to invent, it has not stopped creative minds from doing so. The first poem in palindrome—416 lines long!—was written by Ambrose Hieromonachus Pamperes in 1802.

Interestingly, the two languages with the heaviest number of palindromes are Finnish and Chinese.

32.

L		
	U	

O O Y
T T
R R

33.

T			
			T

R R R R
A A A T
E E P P
S S

34.

M		D	

A A A C
N N L L
E E E
M M M

35.

			K
	B		

E E E E
A A C C
P P L L
K U

36.

B			
			R

A A A A A
R R R R
E E E
T T

37.

	R		D

E E E E
A A I I
K K M D
T N

38.

D			
			A

A A A A A A
E E R R
T T
M J

39.

			L
	C		
			S

I I I A A
S S S E E
R R
L

40.

F				S
				H
	C			
				D

E E E E
T T T N
S S S H
O O R R
L L A C

Take your time with this one.

WORD LADDERS

A *word ladder*, also known as a *doublet*, is, as its name implies, a "ladder of words." You are given two words that constitute the first and last rungs of the ladder, and the goal is to "evolve" one into the other by changing only one letter at a time. Here's the catch: You have to form a legitimate new word with each change.

✦ Sample Word Ladder

The puzzle was invented by none other than Lewis Carroll. At first he called it a *word link*. To show you how one is solved, let's use one of his originals.

Turn the word *head* into *tail* by changing only one letter at a time, forming a new word each time you do so.

H E A D
H E A L   (change D to L)
T E A L   (change H to T)
T E L L   (change A to L)
T A L L   (change E to A)
T A I L   (change L to I)

The four words created in between the given words (*head* and *tail*) are called links. There were four links in this word ladder. ✦

You are given the number of links required for each puzzle in parentheses, and each puzzle will be progressively harder to solve. By the way, some classic puzzles in this genre are scattered throughout this section.

41. Evolve an ape into a man (with just four links).

APE

_____

_____

_____

_____

MAN

42. Turn flour into bread (with five links). *(Lewis Carroll)*

FLOUR

_____

_____

_____

_____

_____

BREAD

43. Go from sleep to dream (also with five links).

SLEEP

_____

_____

_____

_____

_____

DREAM

44. Change one to two (in six steps).

ONE

_____

_____

_____

_____

_____

_____

TWO

45. Turn black to white (also in six steps). *(Lewis Carroll)*

BLACK

_____

_____

_____

_____

_____

_____

WHITE

46. Change the color blue to pink (with eight links).

BLUE

_____

_____

_____

_____

_____

_____

_____

_____

PINK

47. Get from a river to the shore (in ten steps). *(Lewis Carroll)*

RIVER

_____
_____
_____
_____
_____
_____
_____
_____
_____
_____

SHORE

48. Transform a witch into a fairy. You'll need an incredible twelve links—and possibly a dictionary—along the way.

WITCH

_____
_____
_____
_____
_____
_____
_____
_____
_____
_____
_____
_____

FAIRY

And now, let's add a small twist to the puzzle—a twist added by Carroll himself.

49. Change hate into veil with just three links by introducing a new letter (as you have been doing) each time or by rearranging the letters of the word at any step (that is, by anagrammatizing them). You may not do both in the same step.

HATE

_____

_____

_____

VEIL

50. Change iron into lead using the same technique, without knowing how many links are required.

IRON

LEAD

9
CROSSWORDS AND TRIVIA

An average English word is four letters and a half. By hard, honest
labor I've dug all the large words out of my vocabulary and
shaved it down till the average is three and a half.

MARK TWAIN

THE CROSSWORD PUZZLE WAS CREATED by an Englishman named Arthur Wynne. As editor of the "Fun" section of the *New York World,* Wynne introduced what he called a Word Cross on December 21, 1913, after having seen something similar in England. The title "Cross-Word" (hyphenated) came a couple of weeks later, due to a typo. That name stuck, and the puzzle caught on instantly. Readers inundated Wynne with requests for more crosswords. Overnight the puzzle became a craze in New York. By 1924 crosswords had become a pastime. In that year, Simon & Schuster printed the first book compilations of such puzzles. Each book came with a pencil, an eraser and a penny postcard, which puzzle fans could mail to the publisher to request the answers. The first three books alone sold nearly half a million copies. To take advantage of the spreading crossword mania, manufacturers soon began making jewelry, dresses, ties and shoes with crossword designs on them. A song called "Crossword Mama, You Puzzle Me, but Papa's Gonna Figure You Out" also came out in 1924.

Crosswords and trivia games are really all about bringing together bits and pieces of knowledge into a framework. This chapter will challenge you by starting you off with ten crossword puzzles known as *frameworks*. The remaining forty puzzles will test your knowledge of trivia. To make matters even more interesting, you will have to get at the trivia by solving different kinds of puzzles, so your final brain workout will activate various brain areas in tandem.

FRAMEWORKS

Frameworks are similar to regular crosswords, the one difference being that fewer letters cross each word to help you fill in the blanks. These frameworks start out easy, but become increasingly difficult as fewer clues are given in the later puzzles.

1.

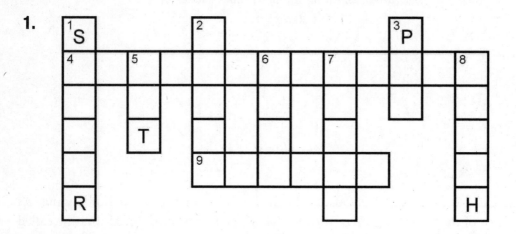

CLUES

1. "Return to ____" (Elvis hit)
2. Way for a baby to get around
3. Writing implement
4. Amusement
5. Toddler
6. Music and literature, for example
7. At no time
8. It's no lie
9. Pay attention to

2.

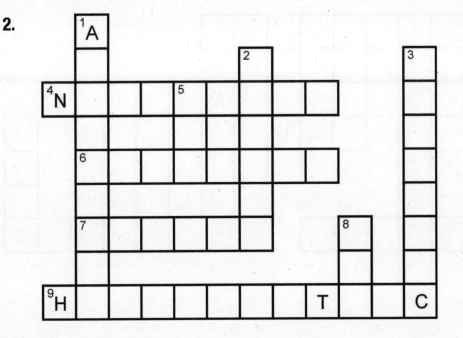

CLUES

1. Greek philosopher who was Plato's student
2. Elementary, middle or high
3. Monthly utility bill
4. He said, "God is dead."
5. Chaotic place or a home for some animals
6. The study of religion
7. Excitement
8. Automobile
9. Having the sun as the center

3.

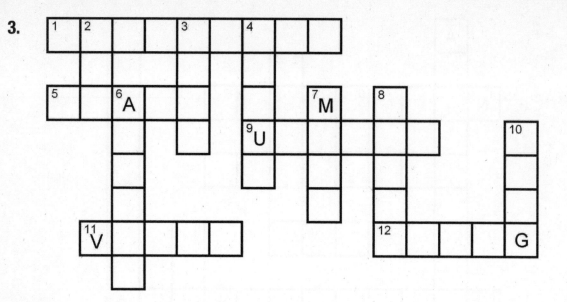

CLUES

1. Famous composer who was deaf
2. Doctor who treats your sinuses (abbr.)
3. Back of the foot
4. Where a trial is held
5. Aver
6. Hunter's trophy
7. God of war
8. Humorous
9. Father of the Titans
10. "I Got Rhythm" or "Happy Birthday"
11. One of tennis's Williams sisters
12. Immature

WORDPLAY

Patrick Creadon's 2006 documentary *Wordplay* is an entertaining look at the world of competitive crossword puzzle solving. It stars Will Shortz, puzzle editor of the *New York Times* and founder of the annual American Crossword Puzzle Tournament. The movie tracks Shortz's lifelong interest in puzzles and profiles some of the greatest crossword solvers as they prepare for the tournament. It also features many well-known crossword aficionados, including former President Bill Clinton, *Daily Show* host Jon Stewart, filmmaker Ken Burns, and New York Yankee star Mike Mussina.

4.

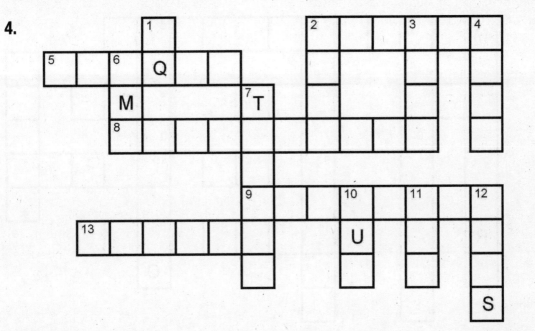

CLUES

1. Kind of test for Mensa membership
2. Where you do the crawl or butterfly (down) / Contemplate (across)
3. Say no to a request
4. Got up
5. Like no other
6. Mischievous child
7. Prevent, as an attack
8. Study of the mind
9. Friendly
10. Kind of card an actor may use
11. It hits the ball out of the park.
12. Completes
13. Ballerina

5.

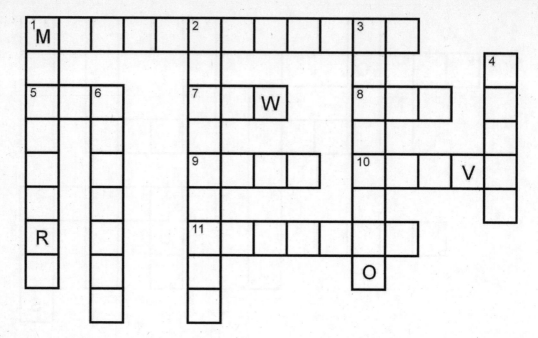

CLUES

1. He painted the Sistine Chapel (across) / Ordinary (down)
2. Great duration of life
3. DiCaprio or Da Vinci
4. Provide food for a wedding
5. A fox's home
6. Nil
7. Novel
8. Aged
9. Tied
10. Breathing
11. Comprise

So far the clues have been numbered for easy scanning as to where the answers go in the grid. The next framework crosswords, however, do not provide this kind of support. You will simply have to figure out where to place the answers to the clues on your own. These are much more difficult, but each puzzle revolves around a theme, which will help you narrow your choices.

6.

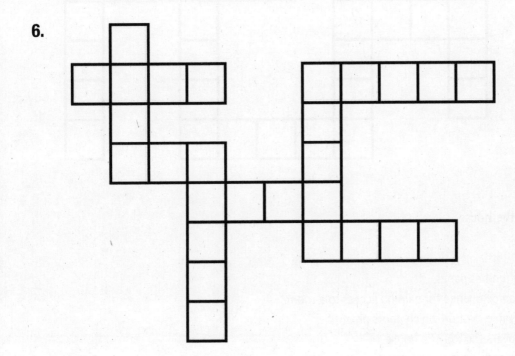

Opposites *(Find the opposite of each given clue.)*

CLUES

1. bad
2. old
3. night
4. timid
5. under
6. stop
7. cloudy
8. false

7.

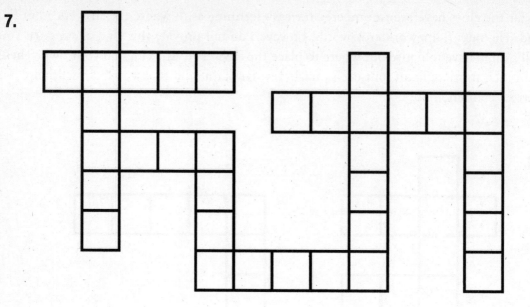

Around the house

CLUES

1. It often has panes.
2. It can be opened for gaining access to a room.
3. Movable joint on which doors pivot
4. It covers the top of a house.
5. A carpet sometimes covers it.
6. Part of a dresser or desk
7. Place to put the car
8. Room below ground

8.

Fun and games

CLUES

1. In this game, players act out the clues.
2. Game in which the object is to jump over pieces and remove them from the board
3. It is the subject of the movie *Searching for Bobby Fischer.*
4. Game in which players make words by placing tiles on a board
5. Type of puzzles that comprise this chapter
6. A variant of rummy, the goal being to gather groups of seven similar cards
7. Card game played alone
8. TV quiz show in which contestants come up with the questions rather than the answers
9. Card game in which players sometimes bluff

9.

Scientists

CLUES

1. Born in Pisa in 1564, he is called the founder of modern experimental methods.
2. Famous for the theory of relativity
3. British scientist who was a coinventor of the calculus, along with Leibniz
4. Italian-born American physicist who produced the first nuclear reaction in 1942
5. He invented the radio.
6. He was so excited by a discovery that he ran naked into the street shouting, "Eureka!"
7. Coined the phrase "the music of the spheres"; also proved a famous theorem

10.

All about love

CLUES

1. Patron saint of love
2. Traditional love gift (often consisting of roses)
3. Love and _____ go together, as a famous song tells us
4. Love without sexual relations, based purely on affection
5. What you send to wedding guests
6. Postwedding vacation
7. "You were always on my _____ ," says a well-known song.
8. "Love me _____ " is the title of an Elvis song.
9. What lovers do often on the lips.

MOVIES

Are you a movie buff? Match the name of each movie star in the left column with the two movies in which he or she has acted in the right column.

11. Harrison Ford

Desperately Seeking Susan

Citizen Kane

12. Madonna

Grumpier Old Men

Mata Hari

13. Orson Welles

Cat Ballou

Interview with the Vampire

14. Sophia (Sofia) Loren

The Deer Hunter

Malcolm X

15. Greta Garbo

The Color Purple

A League of Their Own

16. Jane Fonda

Sister Act

The Bone Collector

17. Tom Cruise

Music of the Heart

Eyes Wide Shut

18. Denzel Washington

Star Wars

The Morning After

19. Whoopi Goldberg

Grand Hotel

Raiders of the Lost Ark

20. Meryl Streep

Two Women

Touch of Evil

Now test your knowledge of movie directors, with an "odd-one-out" puzzle format. For each director, there are four movie choices. Of these, identify the one that was not directed by that director.

21. Steven Spielberg

Schindler's List
Jaws
Jurassic Park
Alien

22. Alfred Hitchcock

Seven
Spellbound
Psycho
Frenzy

23. Federico Fellini

Juliet of the Spirits
The City of Women
Death in Venice
8 ½

24. Stanley Kubrick

History of Violence
Eyes Wide Shut
2001
A Clockwork Orange

25. George Lucas

Star Wars
American Graffiti
The Fly
THX 1138

26. Woody Allen

The Odd Couple
Bananas
Annie Hall
Sweet and Lowdown

27. Jean-Luc Godard

Breathless
Alphaville
A Woman Is a Woman
Spellbound

28. Ingmar Bergman

Wild Strawberries
The Seventh Seal
Open City
Persona

29. Jodie Foster

Tales from the Darkside
Enchanted
Little Man Tate
Home for the Holidays

30. Spike Lee

School Daze
Boyz N the Hood
Four Little Girls
Malcolm X

The next twenty puzzles are in acrostic form. In literature, an acrostic is defined as a poem in which certain letters in each line, taken in order, spell a hidden word or phrase. The puzzle version of the acrostic here involves answering given clues correctly, each of which relates to a famous place, an opera composer and so on. Insert the letters of each answer separately in the appropriate squares. When you have answered all the clues, you will be able to read the name of the answer from top to bottom, in the outlined column. You will be told, at the start, what you are looking for, such as a place or a composer.

Most of the puzzles provide letter clues here and there. Even if you know the answer after solving a few clues, continue filling in the answers to the rest of the clues. Figuring out the clues is part of the puzzle workout—not just getting the acrostic answer.

31.

1		V				I	
2	X						R
3		P	L				
4							
5							
6	C	O				C	

A city

CLUES

1. This composer, famous particularly for his four violin concertos known as *The Four Seasons* (1725), was born there.
2. Marco Polo was also born there. What was he?
3. The city is a port, like this other Italian city on the Mediterranean coast.
4. It is part of this country.
5. There are no roads in the city, just these.
6. Tourism is its chief _____ activity today.

32.

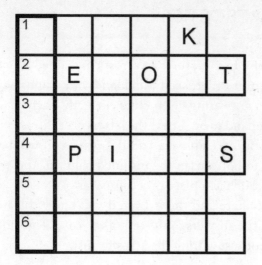

A country

CLUES

1. Main language spoken there
2. In 1814, merchants of this country, living in the Russian empire of the era, organized this kind of movement against the Ottomans.
3. The country's main currency
4. A small, sparsely populated region in the northwest part of the country
5. Located in the Mediterranean Sea, this is the country's largest island.
6. Continent on which this country is found

33.

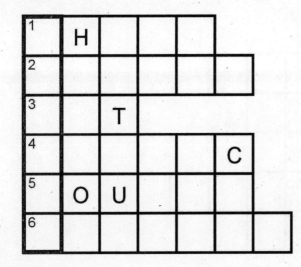

A desert

CLUES

1. The Barbary species of this animal make their homes in its rocky plateaus.
2. It stretches 3,500 miles across the northern part of this continent.
3. Type of climate characteristic throughout this desert region
4. Its name is derived from a word meaning "desert" in this language.
5. Camel caravans continue to cross the desert along ancient _____.
6. It covers a part of this North African country.

34.

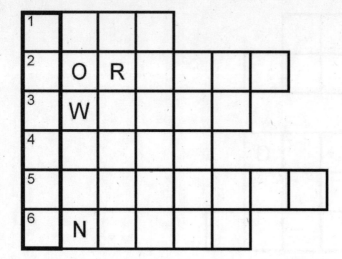

A continent

CLUES

1. Only this other continent covers a larger area and has more people.
2. It has about a fourth of the world's _____.
3. An independent country on this continent
4. One of the religions found on the continent
5. In the early 1900s, most of its regions were empires of this type, controlled by Europeans.
6. Another independent country on this continent

35.

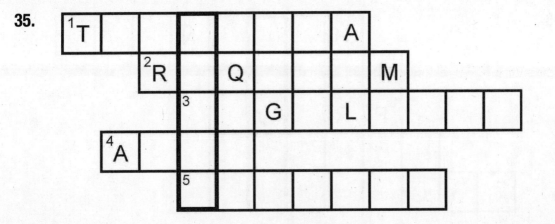

An opera composer

CLUES

1. Probably his most popular opera, about a courtesan named Violetta, who falls tragically in love with Alfredo
2. He also composed one of these masses for the death of his friend, the writer Alessandro Manzoni.
3. This opera is about the tragic story of a hunchback jester.
4. A grand opera that takes place in ancient Egypt
5. Nationality of the composer

36.

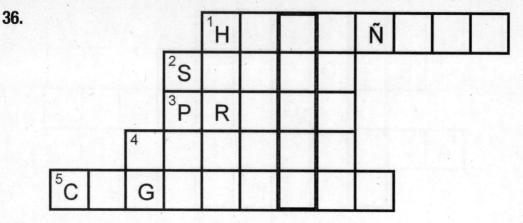

Another opera composer

CLUES

1. Probably the most popular of the arias in the answer to clue 4 that everybody still recognizes today. It is also the name of a dance that originated in Cuba.
2. Country where the opera indicated in clue 4 takes place.
3. At age fourteen, he won first _____ for piano playing.
4. His most famous opera and one of the most popular operas of all time
5. Type of factory in which the heroine of clue 4 works.

37.

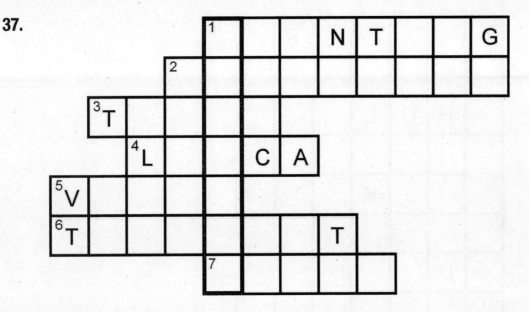

One more opera composer

CLUES

1. In one of his most popular operas, about bohemian life, the character Marcello exercises this artistic profession.
2. Name of a famous opera he composed, *Madama* _____, about a geisha who falls in love with an American naval officer
3. Opera whose chief characters—a famous singer and her painter lover—are persecuted by a villainous chief of police, named Scarpia.
4. City where the composer was born
5. He is considered the operatic heir of this other great opera composer.
6. Opera the composer was working on when he died. The unfinished last scene was completed by another composer.
7. Composer's country of birth

38.

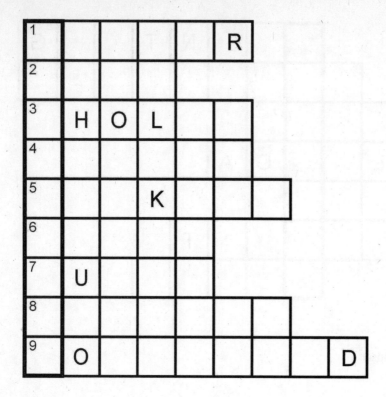

An American state

CLUES

1. Its longest season (in most years)
2. In 1837, Burlington was the state's capital. Burlington is now in this nearby state.
3. This person, who moved to the state, invented the first practical typewriter. His first name is Christopher.
4. This is famous among its dairy products.
5. In this town, one can find an art and an aircraft museum.
6. There are many paper mills in this part of the state.
7. The state tree is this type of maple.
8. It is part of the Midwest, as is this "Hoosier" state.
9. One of the state's colleges

39.

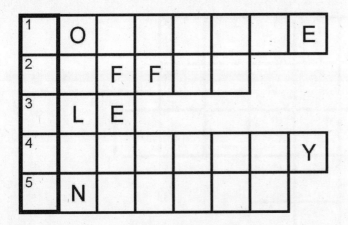

1. ⬜ O ⬜ ⬜ ⬜ ⬜ ⬜ E
2. ⬜ ⬜ F F ⬜ ⬜
3. ⬜ L E ⬜
4. ⬜ ⬜ ⬜ ⬜ ⬜ ⬜ ⬜ Y
5. ⬜ N ⬜ ⬜ ⬜ ⬜ ⬜

A river

CLUES

1. This academic landmark can be found along the left bank of this river.
2. This famous tower can also be found on its left bank.
3. The _____ *de la cité* (Island of the City) is in the river.
4. It winds through this province, where Joan of Arc once fought as a leader of French troops.
5. Its mouth is in the _____ Channel near Le Havre.

40.

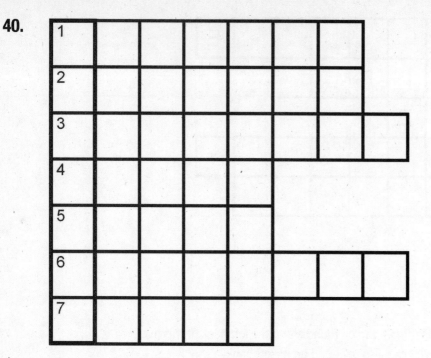

A city *(In this last acrostic puzzle, there are no letter clues at all.)*

CLUES

1. The many farms outside the city also make light industrial products, such as these containers.
2. This type of ruler once governed there.
3. Both the so-called Forbidden City and the _____ City lie within it.
4. The May Fourth Movement was aimed against this country.
5. The city consists of two large areas, one of which is called the _____ City.
6. The city lies on a plain in this region of China.
7. The _____ Hall of the People borders the main square of the city.

Try your hand at guessing who the writer is by means of cryptograms. This time, you will have to solve all ten puzzles simultaneously, going back and forth among them. The reason for this back-and-forthing is that a specific number will correspond to a specific letter in all the cryptograms. For example, if you establish that 1 = H in any one of the ten puzzles, then you can go ahead and substitute *H* for each occurrence of the digit 1 in all the remaining puzzles.

Each cryptogram hides the name and surname of a famous writer. The three given clues relate either to the writer or to his or her works.

41.

___ ___ ___   ___ ___ ___ ___ ___

  1   2   3   4   5   6   7   3

CLUES

1. He wrote a runaway best-seller in 2004 based on a secret code.
2. The book was made into a movie that was directed by Ron Howard.
3. One of his books dealt with the secret society known as the Illuminati.

42.

___ ___ ___ ___ ___ ___ ___   ___ ___ ___ ___ ___ ___ ___

  8   9   2   5 10 11 12   1 13   8 14 11   3 12

CLUES

1. One of his characters is Ebenezer Scrooge.
2. One of his books revolved around the French Revolution.
3. He wrote *Oliver Twist*.

43.

___ ___ ___ ___ ___ ___ ___ ___   ___ ___ ___ ___ ___

15 13 5 16 13 3 13 2   7 6 6 10 17

CLUES

1. She used a literary technique called "stream of consciousness" to write.
2. *To the Lighthouse* is her most famous novel.
3. She belonged to the Bloomsbury Group, a group of intellectuals.

44.

___ ___ ___ ___ ___ ___   ___ ___ ___ ___ ___ ___

18 5 19 20 2 3   8 2 21 6 18 11

CLUES

1. He was the topic of several blockbuster movies at the beginning of the twenty-first century.
2. *In Cold Blood* is his best-known work.
3. In his day, he was a leading celebrity.

45.

—— —— ——   —— —— —— —— —— —— ——

10 11 6   18 6 10 12 18 6 22

CLUES

1. He is one of Russia's greatest writers.
2. His two novel masterpieces are *Anna Karenina* and *War and Peace*.
3. His best-known drama is *The Power of Darkness*.

46.

—— —— —— ——   —— —— —— ——

2 3 3 11   5 13 8 11

CLUES

1. Her novels are often about vampires.
2. Her name is an eponym of an edible grain.
3. One of her novels became a blockbuster 1994 movie, starring Tom Cruise and Brad Pitt.

47.

__ __ __ __ __   __ __ __ __ __ __ __ __ __

11   20   13   10   22   1   13   8   14   13   3   12   6   3

CLUES

1. Many of her poems reflect the disaffection caused by the Civil War.
2. She wrote over seventeen hundred poems.
3. One of her best-known poems, *A Route of Evanescence*, describes the fluttering of a hummingbird.

48.

__ __ __ __   __ __ __ __ __ __ __

20   2   22   2   2   3   16   11   10   6   19

CLUES

1. Probably her best-known work is the first part of her autobiography, *I Know Why the Caged Bird Sings.*
2. Her family name was Marguerite Johnson. Her brother gave her the name she uses.
3. Her poetry explores the experience of being an African American.

49.

— — — — —   — — — — — —

2 10 13 8 11   7 2 10 14 11 5

CLUES

1. She wrote *The Color Purple*, for which she won a Pulitzer Prize in 1983.
2. She became a major figure in feminism, which she called *womanism*.
3. She was born in Eatonton, Georgia.

50.

— — — — — —   — — — — — —

5 6 4 11 5 18   10 19 1 10 19 20

CLUES

1. His plots revolve around espionage, terrorism, conspiracies and corruption at high levels of government.
2. He wrote a best-selling trilogy of novels about a spy named Jason Bourne.
3. He also wrote under the pseudonym Jonathan Ryder.

Answers

CHAPTER 1

1.

```
G R E E N S U O P C C U R
Q W R T A T G H U R B P E
A O R A N G E O R O R C D
S L L O D V P H P W O P D
D L U I E A G U L N W P B
Y E L L O W G H E I N P L
G Y I I O E B N T D C C A
H H S O I N D I G O A L C
W A S B L U E C S D C C K
B R T Y U I L U E D V B M
C A D W H I T E S C A D S
```

2.

```
G R A N D M O T H E R C A
M O T H E R O F A T H E R
D S G H J K L O P M N P R
B R O T H E R T N M N A E
A S C D C A D S P E E R E
S I S T E R G M N R P C C
C A D S L L S N N S H A E
T N U A D E G M P R E D I
C A D S L L D M N C W S N
E L C N U P T R U S M L U
G R A N D F A T H E R I A
```

3.

```
H A R E Y R T S I M E H C
V I G E O M E T R Y Y A G
D C S A C A D S E A P Y E
B O R T N M O L A T H G O
A M O R O C A D S L Y O G
L R T Y Y R L Y G O S L R
N O L G T A Y D E Y I O A
A R I T H M E T I C C I P
L A N G U A G E Y G S B H
A S T R O N O M Y L L D Y
L I T E R A T U R E L U C
```

4.

```
R H F I B R A N C H I H M
B O L B G G H H U U T E T
N M O C A D S L L D T M D
M D W T M D M D L S R P S
W R E G S G R S B R E N E
E C R H T R E D D C E C V A
E A A P S B R A N H R U A
D S H S H R U B T E G O E
C A D S S H R T R D G R L
A S N M T S S A R G L O I
D G H T U O P R B E M T R
```

5.

```
R E K S K L P T S W M V N
D R M O U S E T E T E T A
R D M F M N T R T R M R V
L A P T O P B E I E O E I
L P O W D L N F S F R F G
L P O A G P M G B G Y G A
O H A R D W A R E R D M T
R D M E G P M G W L D E E
C A D S L L D E M D W E V
C H A T R O O M L P O R P
E L G O O G M P B L O G Q
```

6.

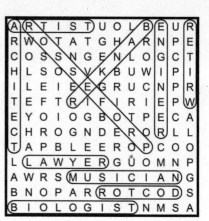

```
A R T I S T U O L B E U R
R W O T A T G H A R N P E
C O S S N G E N L O G C T
H L S O S V K B U W I P I
I L E I E G R U C N P R R
T E F T R I F I R I E P W
E Y O I O G B O T P E C A
C H R O G N D E R O R L L
T A P B L E E R O P C O O
L L A W Y E R G U O M N P
A W R S M U S I C I A N G
B N O P A R R O T C O D S
B I O L O G I S T N M S A
```

The hidden words are: *artist, professor* (diagonal), *banker* (diagonal), *engineer, writer, architect, lawyer, musician, doctor, biologist.*

7.

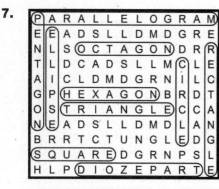

```
P A R A L L E L O G R A M
E E A D S L L D M D G R E
N L S O C T A G O N D R R
T L D C A D S L L M C L E
A I C L D M D G R N I L C
G P H E X A G O N B R D T
O S T R I A N G L E C C A
N E A D S L L D M D L A N
B R R T C T U N G L E D G
S Q U A R E D G R N P S L
H L P D I O Z E P A R T E
```

The hidden words are: *triangle, square, circle, rectangle, ellipse, hexagon, octagon, trapezoid, pentagon, parallelogram.*

8.

```
W A L K N P S R T D P P A
B N M K L F P T N E Y R C
J L B N R J E L I C P O C
U L L R U R E R R E U C E
M T L N N S D P P L R E L
P L L Q I N T P S E M E E
C A D S T M M A P R H D R
L C A D S R D F R A S C A
L L C A D S O T V T N Y T
L D E C A D S T T E I M E
B S C A M P E R E S T P O
```

The hidden words are: *run, trot* (diagonal), *scamper, speed, decelerate, walk, proceed, sprint, jump, accelerate.*

9.

```
A R S C D R C A D S L C L
N E W S P A P E R M D I I
R C D P T D W W I N M N N
N O Q N O I S I V E L E T
W R Y Y P O C A D S L M E
M D N B V C X Z S C D A R
P N Y T S A E O U A L L N
M A G A Z I N E B B N K E
N B V C X Z S T Y L V O T
P N Y T S A E O U E R O G
C O M P U T E R Q W I B K
```

The hidden words are: *newspaper, radio, television, Internet, magazine, book, record, cinema, computer, cable.*

10.

```
Q S R E B O T T L E P O N
B P C A D S L L D M D H A
F O R K C A D S L N T O P
N O N N A D S L L A N P N
M N M I S L L D M P M E M
P R P F L L D M D K P N P
C Q C E L D M D H I C E C
A W A T B N M L P N A R A
D T D Y E T A L P X D R D
S Y S I B N M L P X S R S
T O O T H P I C K X B R E
```

The hidden words are: *spoon, fork, opener, toothpick, plate, bottle, pot, pan, napkin, knife.*

11. Answer: *problems*

R	R	O	P	P	E
P	R	O	P	E	R

L	A	B	N	D
B	L	A	N	D

E	B	M	L	M	E
E	M	B	L	E	M

I	S	M	P	L	E
S	I	M	P	L	E

12. Answer: *headache*

V	E	N	H	E	A
H	E	A	V	E	N

B	I	A	D	E
A	B	I	D	E

V	A	T	R	A	A
A	V	A	T	A	R

H	E	M	C	I	S	T	R	Y
C	H	E	M	I	S	T	R	Y

13. Answer: *quest*

E	S	T	Q	I	O	N	U
Q	U	E	S	T	I	O	N

A	T	E	E	S	T
E	S	T	A	T	E

P	L	E	S	I	M
S	I	M	P	L	E

R	E	C	T	R	C	O
C	O	R	R	E	C	T

14. Answer: *scrooge*

T	A	R	M	S
S	M	A	R	T

E	A	S	E	C	R	I	N
I	N	C	R	E	A	S	E

H	O	O	S	C	L
S	C	H	O	O	L

M	E	G	E	O	T	R	Y
G	E	O	M	E	T	R	Y

15. Answer: *chocolate*

CHNI
I N C H

OCCSER
S O C C E R

CLLEOCT
C O L L E C T

TENATTINO
A T T E N T I O N

16. Answer: *memorabilia*

MOCMEMROATE
C O M M E M O R A T E

TARNIG
R A T I N G

ITYLABI
A B I L I T Y

AILSONI
L I A I S O N

17. Answer: *spaghetti*

ECTASP
A S P E C T

ALLCING
C A L L I N G

PAHPINSSE
H A P P I N E S S

TIONNINET
I N T E N T I O N

18. Answer: *curtains*

PLECOMTE
C O M P L E T E

MMERSUITME
S U M M E R T I M E

NAITCON
C O N T A I N

WERSAN
A N S W E R

19. Answer: *ballet*   **20.** Answer: *numismatics*

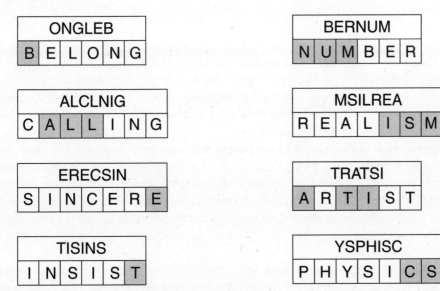

| ONGLEB |
| B E L O N G |

| ALCLNIG |
| C A L L I N G |

| ERECSIN |
| S I N C E R E |

| TISINS |
| I N S I S T |

| BERNUM |
| N U M B E R |

| MSILREA |
| R E A L I S M |

| TRATSI |
| A R T I S T |

| YSPHISC |
| P H Y S I C S |

21. **A bird in the hand is worth two in the bush.** Secret code: Each letter in the proverb is replaced by the one that comes right after it in the alphabet.

22. **Actions speak louder than words.** Secret code: Each letter in the proverb is replaced by the one that comes right before it in the alphabet.

23. *Gone with the Wind.* Secret code: Each letter in the title is replaced by the second letter that comes after it in the alphabet.

24. **I think, therefore I am.** Secret code: Each letter in the saying (by René Descartes) is replaced by the fourth letter that comes after it in the alphabet.

25. *All's Well That Ends Well.* Secret code: A number is assigned to each letter as it occurs in the title in order. Thus, *A* is the first letter to appear and is assigned the number 1; *L* is the second letter to appear and is assigned the number 2; and so on. When *A* appears again, it is replaced by the number 1; when *L* appears again, it is replaced by the number 2 and so on.

26. **Bad art is a great deal worse than no art at all.** Secret code: The letter *A* is the first letter of the alphabet, so it is encoded as the first number 1 (if *A* occurs in the quotation); the letter *B* is the second letter, so it is encoded as the second number 2 (if *B* occurs in the quotation) and so on. In sum: *A* = 1, *B* = 2, *C* = 3, *D* = 4 and so on. Since not all the letters of the alphabet occur in the quotation, some numbers appear to have been skipped, so to speak, in the cryptogram.

27. Great bodies of people are never responsible for what they do. Secret code: The five vowels in order are *A, E, I, O, U*. The first five numbers have been used to replace these in that order: *A* = 1, *E* = 2, *I* = 3, *O* = 4, *U* = 5.

28. Life is a bridge. Cross over it, but build no house on it. Secret code: As in puzzle 25, a number is assigned to each consonant as it occurs in the title in order. Thus, *L* is the first consonant to appear and is assigned the number 1; *F* is the second consonant to appear and is assigned the number 2 and so on. When *L* appears again, it is replaced by the number 1; when *F* appears again, it is replaced by the number 2 and so on.

29. If you have only one smile in you, give it to the people you love. Secret code: The five vowels are replaced by the first five numbers: *A* = 1, *E* = 2, *I* = 3, *O* = 4, *U* = 5. As for the consonants, the same encrypting technique as the one in puzzles 25 and 28 has been used. A number, starting from 6 (since the first five have been used up for the vowels) is assigned to each consonant as it occurs in the quotation in order. Thus, *F* is the first consonant to appear and is assigned the number 6; *Y* is the second consonant to appear and is assigned the number 7 and so on.

30. Flattery makes friends and truth makes enemies. Secret code: The first letter of the alphabet is assigned the first number: *A* = 1. The second letter of the alphabet is assigned the second number: *B* = 2. And so on up to *I* = 9. All letters after that have not been encrypted. Moreover, if a letter before *I* does not occur, then the relevant number is skipped as well. For example, the letter *B* does not occur and thus the number 2 is not used.

31. Only *blame* does not contain the cluster *sp* in its structure.

32. All words except *blue* refer to a shade, tinge or hue of red.

33. All words except *plain* have four letters in them.

34. *Orange* is a fruit, while all the other words refer to vegetables.

35. All the words except *cube* refer to things that have a spherical shape.

36. All the words except *try* begin with a vowel.

37. All the words except *catch* end with the cluster *nd*.

38. All the words except *clay* refer to liquids or anything that has liquid properties.

39. All the words except *easy* have two *a*'s in them.

40. All the words except *pole* refer to containers.

41. Pun. Pattern: In each three-letter word, only the initial consonant is different; the remaining two letters **(un)** remain constant throughout the sequence.

42. Connect. Pattern: Each word has a double consonant in it **(rr, mm, tt, ss, nn).**

43. Nice. Pattern: Each word has four letters in it.

44. Build. Pattern: The letters in a word increase in numerical order (**I** = one-letter word, **am** = two-letter word, **two** = three-letter word and so on).

45. Guy. Pattern: Each word refers to a male.

46. Movies. Pattern: The words, if joined, will form a sentence **(The girl loves watching movies).**

47. Galileo. Pattern: Each word is a clue related to Galileo, who was a scientist, an Italian and an inventor and whose theories were considered controversial at the time.

48. Mom. Pattern: Each word can be read forward and backward. By the way, such a word is called a **palindrome.**

49. Engaged. Pattern: The words start with the letters of the alphabet in order **(A, B, C, D, E).**

50. Crabby. Pattern: This was a tough one! The only vowel in each word is **A.** The number of consonants in each successive word surrounding **A** increases by one: **at** = one consonant, **par** = two consonants and so on.

CHAPTER 2

1. If you stare at the image, you will at one moment see a vase or goblet and at another the profile of two faces looking at each other. The image pattern alternates back and forth in your mind as you continue to look.

2. The four lines are upright (perpendicular). The slanted lines crossing them trick the eye into seeing the upright lines as slanting slightly as well.

3. The lines are actually the same length. Line AB looks longer because the brain interprets the chevrons (arrowheads) orienting outward as extending its length and, vice versa, line CD looks shorter because the brain interprets the chevrons orienting inward as decreasing its length.

4. The lines are equal.

5. The lines are parallel. But because they are juxtaposed against a background of lines that radiate from the dot and that intersect the two parallel lines, the brain is tricked into believing that they bulge.

6. If you stare at the figure, you will see at one moment a three-pronged fork and at another a two-pronged fork. In other words, the contours of the lines in the figure do double visual duty within it.

7. If you stare at the cube, it will spontaneously reverse its depth—that is, you will find it impossible to fix the front and back of the figure in your mind. They seem to flip back and forth spontaneously.

For puzzles 8–20, no visual explanations are given after puzzle 8. If you do not understand an answer, go back to the specific puzzle and look, look, look, look again! If you still cannot come up with the answer, you might have to imitate the style of visual explanation provided for puzzle 8.

8. seven

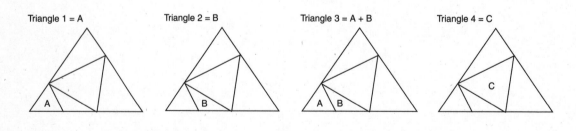

Triangle 1 = A   Triangle 2 = B   Triangle 3 = A + B   Triangle 4 = C

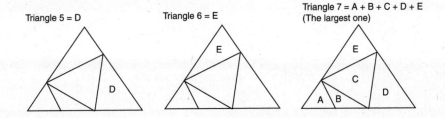

Triangle 5 = D

Triangle 6 = E

Triangle 7 = A + B + C + D + E
(The largest one)

9. twelve

10. seven

11. five

12. ten

13. eighteen

14. sixty

15. twenty-three

16. As incredibly complicated as the diagram appears, there are only six circles in it.

17. ninety

18. The hidden word is *illusion*.

```
I  I  I  I  I  I  L  L  L  L  L  L  I  L  L  S  S  S  U
L  L  L  L  I  L  I  I  L  U  U  S  I  N  I  O  S  I  U
L  L  L  L  I  L  L  L  L  I  U  S  O  O  S  S  S  U
L  U  U  S  I  N  O  L  L  L  I  U  S  O  O  O  S  I  U
L  U  U  S  I  N  O  U  U  U  U  U  U  N  S  S  S  U
L  U  U  S  I  N  O  S  S  S  S  S  S  O  O  S  I  U
I  I  I  I  I  I  I  L  I  L  L  I  U  S  O  O  S  S  S  U
L  U  U  S  I  N  O  O  L  L  I  U  S  O  O  O  S  I  U
L  U  U  S  I  N  O  N  L  L  I  U  S  O  O  U  S  O  O
I  I  I  I  I  I  L  L  L  L  L  L  I  L  L  S  S  S  U
```

19. one hundred

20. thirty-five

21. 2. Pattern: Each figure has one more line in it than the previous one.

22. 1. Pattern: The two lines within a rectangle follow this alternating pattern: slanted, upright, slanted, upright and so on.

23. 1. Pattern: The two lines within each pair of figures follow this alternating pattern: crossing upright (to the line of sight), crossing at an angle (to the line of sight) and so on.

24. 2. Pattern: The arrow is rotating in a clockwise fashion—each rotation is 90°.

25. 2. Pattern: If you look closely, you will see that the arrowhead is rotating in a counterclockwise fashion—each rotation is 90°.

26. 1. Pattern: Each square has one more line in it than the previous one.

27. 1. Pattern: Both lines are rotating back and forth at 90°.

28. 2. Pattern: Each triplet of figures (no matter what their orientation) alternates as follows: two white, two black, two white, two black and so on. So the next figure set must have two white figures in it.

29. 2. Pattern: Every figure that occurs in an odd-numbered position (first, third, etc.) has no underline; every figure that occurs in an even-numbered position (second, fourth, etc.) does.

30. 1. Pattern: Every figure that occurs in an odd-numbered position (first, third, etc.) is made up of straight lines; every figure that occurs in an even-numbered position (second, fourth, etc.) is a curve of some kind.

31. There are several possibilities. Below is one of them.

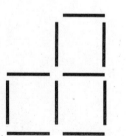

32. If you join the first two sticks into a V-shape, you will get the Roman numeral for eight.

33. Below is one solution; there are others.

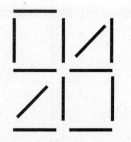

34. The addition below (made with the four sticks) produces two.

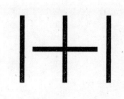

35. You can get one by forming a square root sign or a multiplication sign as shown. The square root of one is one, and one times one is also one.

$$\sqrt{1}$$
$$1 \times 1$$

36. If you unite the last two sticks into a V-shape, you will get the Roman numeral for four.

37. Here's how to get one-half in Roman numerals.

$$\frac{I}{II}$$

38. If you make the sticks cross, you will get the Roman numeral for ten.

39. Move one stick as shown to get the square root sign. The figure now represents one over the square root of one, which equals one.

40.

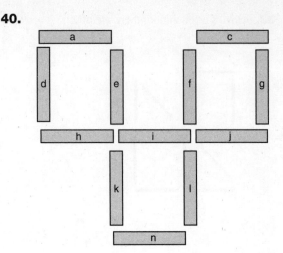

41. Nineteen. If you do not see it, make yourself a model of the figure with billiard balls and try it out for yourself.

42. thirty-eight

43. A occurs in all four circles, B in two, C in two and D in three.

44. Although the original strip had two sides, when given a half twist it has only one. To check this, make a similar strip, as described in the puzzle, and draw a line down the middle until you reach the place where you started. You will discover that your line runs around the original two sides of the strip. This is known as the Möbius strip, after August F. Möbius, the German mathematician who discovered it in the mid-1800s.

45. Recall from school geometry that the two diagonals of a rectangle equal each other in length. Let's draw the other diagonal. As you can see, that diagonal is a radius of the circle. Since the latter is equal to 6 inches plus 4 inches, or 10 inches total, and the radii of a circle are equal, the diagonal that was just drawn is also 10 inches long. And since the diagonals of a rectangle are equal, the length of the diagonal AB is thus 10 inches.

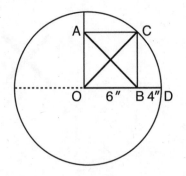

46. A zigzag cut as shown below will do the trick. Then slide the array of pieces down as shown.

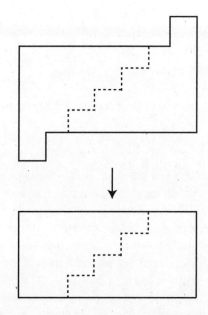

47. It cannot be done. Two squares of the same color have been removed from the board, whereas each domino has two colors on it. You can cover the whole board with black-and-white dominoes if there are black and white pairs of squares on the board to put them on. But the modified board has removed two of the same color, and, thus, you cannot cover the board with dominoes.

48. There is only one place on earth where this can happen—the North Pole. From a North Pole location, which is on top of the globe, the explorer could go south a mile, walk east, and then walk north, and she would be right back where she started from—at the North Pole! If you cannot visualize this, get ahold of a globe and try it out for yourself.

49. You will get one huge haystack. If you cannot visualize this, conduct the following experiment with feathers. In one part of your living room, make three and seven-ninths piles of feathers (approximately, of course). In another part, make two and two-thirds piles of feathers (again, approximately). Now put all the piles together. How many piles of feathers do you now have?

50. Neither train will be nearer to New York than the other. The trick in this puzzle is to visualize what happens when the two trains meet. Everything else in the puzzle is useless information. Consider the point where the two trains cross each other (wherever that may be). By meeting there, both trains are in exactly the same spot. Each is equally distant from New York, albeit pointing in different directions. After meeting at that point, one train goes on to Chicago and the other to New York—the former getting farther and farther away from New York and the latter getting closer and closer.

CHAPTER 3

For puzzles 1–10, you might find patterns other than the ones given.

1. 38. Pattern: Add all the corner numbers and place the result in the center. That's all there is to this one.

2. 80. Pattern: Multiply the corner numbers in any order and place the result in the center.

3. 40. Pattern: Add the top two numbers and place the result in the lower right corner; double that number and place the result in the lower left corner; then double that number as well and place it in the center.

4. 45. Pattern: Start with the upper left number. Double it and insert the result in the lower left corner. Double that number and place the result in the upper right corner, then double that number as well and place it in the lower right corner. Add all four corners and place the result in the center.

5. 13. Pattern: The numbers in the corners increase by one in clockwise fashion from the upper left corner to the lower left corner. Start with the upper left number. Add one to it and insert the result in the upper right corner. Add one to that number and place the result in the lower right corner, then add one to that number as well and place it in the lower left corner. Add one to that number and place it in the center.

6. 20. Pattern: This is an alternating pattern of subtracting three, then adding two. Start by subtracting three from the upper left number and placing the result in the lower left corner. Add two to that number and place the result in the lower right corner. Subtract three from that number and place the result in the upper right corner. Finally, add two to that number and place the result in the center.

7. 75. Pattern: The upper left number multiplies the sum of the other three corner numbers. The result of this whole operation is placed in the center.

8. 49. Pattern: First add the numbers in two diagonal corners together. For the first grid, this would be: 2 + 3 = 5 and 5 + 4 = 9. Multiply the two results together: 5 × 9 = 45. Place the last result in the center.

9. 1. Pattern: Divide the number in the upper left corner by the one below it in the lower left corner. Place the result in the lower right corner. Divide that number by the number in the upper right corner and place the result in the center. In the first grid, for example, here's the sequence: 8 ÷ 2 = 4 and place 4 in the lower-right corner; 4 ÷ 2 = 2 and place 2 in the center.

10. 55. Pattern: First add the corner numbers on the right. For example, in the first grid, 4 + 3 = 7. Next, subtract the numbers in the other two corners. In the first grid, 7 − 5 = 2. Multiply these two results together: 7 × 2 = 14. Place this final result in the center.

11.

Relation	Nickname
Father	Cat
Mother	Bee
Daughter	Wee

12.

Name	Skirt color
Ms. Violet	scarlet
Ms. Scarlet	brown
Ms. Brown	violet

13.

Friend	Cat	Dog
Gina	Benji	Droopy
Barbara	Ruff	Benji
Harry	Mack	Ruff
Danny	Droopy	Mack

14.

Name	Field
Becky	drummer
Pat	singer
Rina	violinist
Sam	pianist

15.

Name	Area of Expertise
Katia	DNA expert
Lina	detective
Maya	criminologist
Johanna	profiler
Pina	anthropologist
Paul	weapons expert

16.

Name	Course
Sandhu	fencing
Hanna	judo
Laura	ballet
Amin	opera

17.

Order	Item
First	notepad
Second	keys
Third	SMS device
Fourth	earphones
Fifth	cell phone

18.

Year	Instrument	City
2006	saxophone	Milwaukee
2007	horn	Orlando
2008	trumpet	Atlanta
2009	clarinet	Denver

19.

Name	iPod Color	Beverage Ordered
Bella	green	tea
Chita	black	juice
Ira	orange	milk
Dina	blue	coffee
Mika	red	soft drink

20.

First Name	Last Name	Item Sold
Amy	Smith	computers
Katia	Kristoff	clothes
Shamila	Armad	jewelry
Renata	Miller	CDs
Henrietta	Cramer	books

Where relevant for puzzles 21–30, the rankings are shown below each answer.

21. Jack is the tallest.
Jack
Maria
Juan
Deb

22. Shauna earns the most and Maggie the least.
Shauna
Bill
Betty
Maggie

23. The winner is Mack.
Mack
Xavier
Jack
Mary
Jessie

24. The winner is Meagan.
Meagan
Sandy
Kathy
Mary
Betty
Cheryl

25. Alex is the tallest and Louise the shortest.
Alex
Sarah
Chris
Danielle
Lucy
Louise

26. Frank is the tallest.
Frank
Dina
Evelyn
Cheryl
Barney
Aaron

27. *E*

28. *E*

29. Jeb is the tallest.
Jeb
Jack
Jen
Jill

30. Hack is the shortest.
Zack
Jack
Mack
Dack
Hack

31. He belongs to the liar clan. The reasoning is the same as in the sample puzzle. If the woman is a truth-teller, she would say so and thus "Goneh" translates as "yes" (truthfully). If she is a liar, she would also say that she belongs to the truth-telling clan, even though it is a lie. Again, "Goneh" thus translates as "yes." The man's statement is a lie, because the woman had in fact answered "yes."

32. The man belongs to the truth-telling clan and the woman to the liar clan. Again, the key to the solution is the fact that the woman's answer to the question, "Goneh," translates as "yes," no matter to which clan she actually belongs. The reasoning is the same as in the sample puzzle and in puzzle 31. The man's statement is obviously true, because the woman had in fact answered "yes." So he told the truth and is, therefore, a truth-teller. Thus, the second part of his statement, "but she is a liar," is also true, and the woman belongs to the liar clan.

33. Using similar reasoning as that used for the previous puzzles, "Buneh" translates as "I am a Tami." If the first villager is indeed a Tami (a truth-teller), he would say so. If he is not, belonging instead to the lying Fami clan, he would also say that he was a Tami. He would not say that he was a Fami, under the circumstances, for that would be the truth. The third villager obviously lied and is thus a member of the Fami clan. The second villager told the truth when he or she remarked about the first one, "He said he was a Tami," so the second villager is a Tami. That same villager also indicated that the first villager lied. So the first villager is a Fami, who lied when he said that he was a Tami.

34. If the first villager is in fact a Fami, she would not admit it, being a strategic liar. So her answer would have been, "No, I am not" (which is a lie). If she is a Tami, she would tell the truth and thus would also answer the question with "No, I am not (a Fami)." The second villager told the truth, so he or she belongs to the Tami clan. The third one clearly lied, so he or she belongs to the Fami clan. It is not possible to determine the clan membership of the first villager.

35. The villager's answer is a lie. Why? Because he or she said that the other two are Tamis, but would not admit that they were Tamis. This is impossible, because Tamis always tell the truth. The first villager is a liar, belonging to the Fami clan. Being a liar, his statement that the other two are Tamis is also a lie. All three villagers are Famis.

36. It cannot be determined if Epimenides spoke the truth or lied. If he spoke the truth, then his statement, "All Cretans are liars," will also be true. But that means that Epimenides, being himself a Cretan, is a liar (as the statement affirms). However, he cannot speak the truth and be a liar at the same time. Let's assume instead that Epimenides lied. Then his statement, "All Cretans are liars," is actually true. Again, Epimenides seems to have both lied and told the truth at the same time. Conclusion? We cannot determine the truth value of Epimenides' statement.

37. It cannot be determined because the assertion made leads to a circularity. If the barber goes ahead and shaves himself, then he has shaved someone in the village who does, in fact, shave himself—namely himself, the barber! If he does not shave himself, then he is leaving out someone in the village who does not shave himself—again, himself, the barber!

38. It is not possible for anyone to make that statement, logically speaking. Here's why. According to his or her statement, the speaker belongs to a village of liars. So whatever he or she says is a lie. But the statement turns out to be true, and thus the statement is a contradiction. Then again, the speaker could be a trickster!

39. It cannot be determined. Let's assume that the box-maker is a truth-teller. His or her inscription ("This box was not made by a liar") is obviously true. Conclusion? The box-maker was indeed a truth-teller. But, to be sure, let's check out the other possible assumption. Let's assume that the box-maker is a liar. Since he or she would never admit that the box was made by a liar (which is what he or she is), the box-maker would also write: "This box was not made by a liar." So, the inscription could also have been written by a liar.

40. The coin is in B. Let's assume that inscription A is true. The upshot would be that the coin is in A. Further, it implies that B's inscription is also true—if the coin is in A, then, as B's inscription proclaims, it is certainly not in B. But this is contrary to the condition that at most one inscription is true. We can thus discard our initial assumption. In the process, however, we have discovered that A's inscription is false—the coin is not in A. That makes C's inscription true, since it merely confirms that the coin is not in A. Since at most only one of the inscriptions is true, then B's inscription ("The coin is not in here.") is false. Since this does not lead to any contradiction, it can be safely concluded that the coin is in B, contrary to what B's inscription says.

For all but the very last puzzle in this set, no elaborations are given. The logic used is straightforward and thus similar to the one used in the sample puzzle.

41. Andrew

42. Garth

43. Doreen

44. Jason

45. Dick

46. Horace

47. Carson

48. Jat

49. Beck

50. Theo is innocent because he says so twice, and one of these must be true because two of the three statements he made are true. If he did it, then both would be false, and this is impossible. Thus, (9) is a lie and (8) is true. Since (8) is true, (15) is a lie and (14) is true. Judy is the thief.

CHAPTER 4

1. Three balls drawn in a row will do the trick. Here's the reasoning behind this solution. Assume that you draw a white ball first and a black one second. So far, no match. But look carefully at what you have—one white ball and one black ball. Put them aside, put the blindfold back on and draw a third ball out. What is its color? There are only two colors that the third ball can be: white or black. If it's white, it matches the white ball already outside the box. If it's black, it matches the black ball already outside the box. Thus, no matter what the color of the third ball is, it will be a match with one of the two balls already outside the box. Note, by the way, that the order of drawing is not relevant.

2. Four balls. The reasoning is the same as before. Assume that on your first three draws, you draw a white ball, a black one and a green one. (The order in which these colors are drawn is irrelevant; the point is that you will draw out three different colors in a "worst-case scenario" situation.) With your blindfold back on, draw a fourth ball out. There are only three colors that the fourth ball can be: white, black or green. Thus, no matter what the color of the fourth ball is, it will be a match with one of the three balls already outside the box.

3. Five balls. The reasoning is the same as before. Assume that on your first four picks, you draw one white ball, one black one, a green one and a red one. (Again, the order in which these four colors are drawn is irrelevant; the point is that you will draw out four balls of four different colors in a worst-case scenario.) With your blindfold back on, draw a fifth ball out. There are only four colors that the fifth ball can be: white, black, green or red. Thus, no matter what the color of the fifth ball is, it will be a match with one of the four balls already outside the box.

Let's summarize the results of the three puzzles.
(1) Number of colors = 2; number of draws required = 3
(2) Number of colors = 3; number of draws required = 4
(3) Number of colors = 4; number of draws required = 5

The general pattern seems to be that you will need to make one more draw than the number of different colors of the balls in the box.

4. Here again, you will need to make one more draw than the number of different colors of the balls in the box, or six draws. Let's go through the reasoning again. Assume that on your first five draws, you pull out one white ball, one black ball, one green one, one red one and one orange ball to complete the worst-case scenario. The order in which these five colors are drawn is irrelevant. With your blindfold back on, draw a sixth ball out. There are five colors that the sixth ball can be: white, black, green, red or orange. No matter what the color of the sixth ball is, it will be a match with one of the five balls already outside the box. And the number of balls in a color does not affect the outcome, unless there was only one ball in a particular color.

5. Thirteen gloves. There are twenty-four gloves in all in the box. Because some gloves fit the right hand and some the left hand, one might pick all twelve left-hand gloves, as a worst-case scenario. However, the thirteenth glove will be a right-handed one (that's all that is left in the box) and will also match one of the previous twelve in color. Thus, in this case, thirteen gloves will have to be drawn to ensure a pair of matching gloves.

6. The answer is seven, and the reasoning is similar to previous puzzles. Assume that you draw a white ball, a black one and a blue one (the order in which these colors are drawn, as you know by now, is irrelevant). With your blindfold back on, draw a fourth ball out. There are only three colors that the third ball can be: white, black or blue. If it's white, it matches the white ball already outside the box. If it's black, it matches the black ball already outside the box. If it's green, it matches the green ball already outside the box. With the fourth draw, you will end up with a pair that matches. Similarly, with a fifth draw, you will end up with a second pair that matches. And with a sixth draw, you will end up with the third pair that matches—all because of the worst-case-scenario condition. Outside the box you now have three matching pairs—two white, two black and two blue. Go back and draw the seventh ball, which will be white, black or blue. Any one of these will match one of the pairs outside the box to produce a matching triplet.

7. First weighing: Put three balls on one pan of the scale and the other three on the other pan. The pan that goes up is the lighter pan and thus contains the culprit ball (the one that weighs less). Eliminate the three good balls so identified. Take the three suspect balls (the ones on the pan that went up). Put one of these in a corner. Put the other two suspect balls on separate pans for the second weighing. If the pans do not budge, then you have identified the culprit ball—it's the one in the corner. If one of the pans goes up, you will also have identified the culprit ball because it's in the pan that went up.

8. Two weighings again. First weighing: Put three balls on one pan of the scale and the other three on the other pan. Put the seventh ball in the corner. If the pans balance, then the culprit ball is the one in the corner. If you're lucky, one weighing will do. Under the worst-case scenario, the pan that goes up is the lighter pan and thus contains the culprit ball. Eliminate the three good balls. Take the three suspect balls (the ones on the pan that went up). Put one of these in a corner. Second weighing: Put the other two suspect balls on separate pans. If the pans do not budge, then you have identified the culprit ball—it's the one in the corner. If one of the pans goes up, you will also have identified the culprit ball because it's in the pan that went up.

9. Three weighings will do the trick. First weighing: Put six balls on one pan of the scale and the other six on the other pan. The pan that goes up is the lighter pan and thus contains the culprit ball. Eliminate the six good balls. Take the six suspect balls (the ones on the pan that went up). Second weighing: Put three of these balls on one pan of the scale and the other three on the other. The pan that goes up from this experiment is the lighter pan and thus contains the culprit ball. Eliminate the three good balls. Take the three suspect balls (the ones on the pan that went up). Put one of these in a corner. Third weighing: Put the other two suspect balls on separate pans. If the pans do not budge, then you have identified the culprit ball—it's the one in the corner. If one of the pans goes up, you will also have identified the culprit ball—it's in the pan that went up.

10. Create three groups of seven balls each. First, weigh any two groups of seven and place the third group in a corner. If one of the two groups is lighter, that group contains the lighter ball. If the two groups balance out equally, the group in the corner contains the lighter ball. For your second weighing, take the group that has been determined to contain the lighter ball, divide it into two groups of three balls each and put the leftover ball in a corner. If the two groups balance, the ball in the corner is the lighter ball and we have a solution. But we cannot assume this, so let's assume that one of the two groups contains the lighter ball. So, as a third weighing, weigh any ball opposite any other ball, leaving the third ball in the corner. If one of these two is lighter, that is the culprit ball. If not, then it is the ball in the corner. Altogether, three weighings are sufficient.

11. Let W = white checker and B = black checker. The given rules of movement are that (1) a checker may be moved over one adjacent checker into an empty space, or else it may be moved one space into an empty space; and (2) W can only move to the right, B to the left. Below is the sequence of moves required.

(0) W __ B *(Starting position)*

(1) __ W B *(W was moved right into the empty space in (0) above).*

(2) B W __ *(B was moved over W into the empty space in (1) above).*

(3) B __ W *(W was moved right into the empty space in (2) above; the positions are now reversed.)*

12. The reasoning is the same as in puzzle 11. The sequence chart of moves below is self-explanatory (W = white checker and B = black checker).

(0) W W __ B B
(1) W __ W B B
(2) W B W __ B
(3) W B W B __
(4) W B __ B W
(5) __ B W B W
(6) B __ W B W
(7) B B W __ W
(8) B B __ W W

13. Here's the sequence chart of moves. As a general rule, note that the solution depends on alternating the combination W B W B wherever possible.

(0) W W W __ B B B
(1) W W __ W B B B
(2) W W B W __ B B
(3) W W B W B __ B
(4) W W B __ B W B
(5) W __ B W B W B
(6) __ W B W B W B
(7) B W __ W B W B
(8) B W B W __ W B
(9) B W B W B W __
(10) B W B W B __ W
(11) B W B __ B W W
(12) B __ B W B W W
(13) B B __ W B W W
(14) B B B W __ W W
(15) B B B __ W W W

209

14. Remove three coins so that the arrangement looks like this:

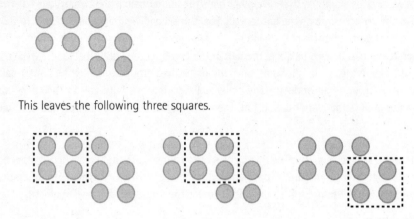

This leaves the following three squares.

15. The traveler starts by bringing across the goat, leaving the wolf and the cabbage on the original side. He reaches the other side, leaves the goat and comes back alone. From the original side, the traveler picks up the wolf, rows to the other side, drops off the wolf and takes the goat back with him. He drops off the goat on the original side and takes the cabbage over with him. At the other side, he leaves the cabbage with the wolf. He goes back alone and picks up the goat from the original side. He rows over to the other side, where he descends with the goat and unites it with the wolf and the cabbage, and continues on his journey.

16. Here's how the back-and-forth crossings might unfold. Each couple is identified with a number: H1 and W1 are a husband-and-wife pair; H2 and W2 are a second husband-and-wife pair; and H3 and W3 are a third husband-and-wife pair. By the way, it does not matter if H2 and W2 or H3 and W3, rather than H1 and W1, were the first to cross; the result would be the same. There are also other possibilities in between, but they all produce versions of the solution given below. As required, at no time is a woman with a different man without her husband being present (on the original side, on the boat or on the other side).

ON THE ORIGINAL SIDE	ON THE BOAT	ON THE OTHER SIDE
(0) H1 W1 H2 W2 H3 W3	__ __	__ __ __ __ __ __
(1) __ __ H2 W2 H3 W3	H1 W1 →	__ __ __ __ __ __
(2) __ __ H2 W2 H3 W3	← __ W1	H1 __ __ __ __ __
(3) __ __ H2 __ H3 W3	W1 W2 →	H1 __ __ __ __ __
(4) __ __ H2 __ H3 W3	← __ W2	H1 W1 __ __ __ __
(5) __ __ __ __ H3 W3	H2 W2 →	H1 W1 __ __ __ __
(6) __ __ __ __ H3 W3	← __ W2	H1 W1 H2 __ __ __
(7) __ __ __ __ H3 __	W2 W3 →	H1 W1 H2 __ __ __
(8) __ __ __ __ H3 __	← __ W3	H1 W1 H2 W2 __ __
(9) __ __ __ __ __ __	H3 W3 →	H1 W1 H2 W2 __ __
(10) __ __ __ __ __ __	__ __	H1 W1 H2 W2 H3 W3

17. First the boys cross the river. One stays; the other boy brings the boat to the soldiers and gets out. One soldier gets in the boat and crosses over. At the other side, the boy who was there brings the boat back to the soldiers. He takes the other boy across to the other shore. One of the boys takes the boat back, gets out, and a second soldier crosses over. This pattern continues until all soldiers have crossed.

18. He is either the boy's father or his uncle.

19. She's the girl's aunt.

20. She's the man's wife.

21. She's the first girl's cousin.

22. He's your father, or your uncle.

23. She's your mother, or your aunt.

24. He's your uncle.

25. She's your aunt.

26. He's your cousin.

27. He's your brother-in-law.

28. She's your sister-in-law.

29. She was the sick boy's mother.

30. The boy says that he has no brothers or sisters, so when he refers to "my father's son," he is referring to himself. Therefore, the man in the photo is his father, and he is that man's son.

31. screen or monitor *(Pens transfer text to paper, keyboards to a screen.)*

32. sky or air *(Boats travel on water, airplanes in the sky.)*

33. brain or mind *(We say that love takes place in the heart and thinking in the brain or the mind.)*

34. beavers *(People make and live in a house, beavers make and live in dams.)*

35. straight (rigid, inflexible, and so on) *(opposites)*

36. far or remote *(synonyms)*

37. fruit *(A tulip is a type of flower; an orange is a type of fruit.)*

38. Paula *(male-female name pairs)*

39. art, painting, drawing or even sculpture *(Literature is all about the creative use of words, art the creative use of figures.)*

40. (golf) courses *(Teachers do their thing in classrooms, golfers on a course.)*

41. seeing *(You need oxygen to breathe and light to see.)*

42. cruelty, meanness and so on

43. two *(A is the first letter and B the second, one is the first natural number and two the second.)*

44. Y *(A is the first letter, Z the last, B is the second letter, Y the second last.)*

45. lady *(Mister is the title used with gentlemen and others, Madam with ladies and others.)*

46. sadness *(Laughter often accompanies happiness, crying sadness.)*

47. death *(Day, like life, starts things off, while night, like death, brings them to an end.)*

48. The box labeled 10¢ contains four nickels (20¢); the box labeled 15¢ contains two nickels (10¢); and the box labeled 20¢ contains three nickels (15¢). Each box is mislabeled; that is, if it says 10¢, then you know for certain that it does not have 10¢ in it, but 15¢ or 20¢. The contents of Box B are revealed to you as being two nickels (10¢). Here are these facts displayed in visual form:

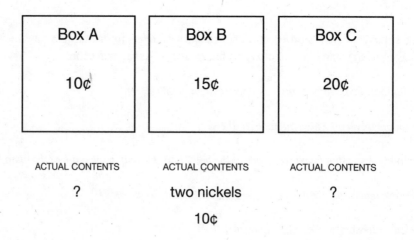

Box A	Box B	Box C
10¢	15¢	20¢

ACTUAL CONTENTS   ACTUAL CONTENTS   ACTUAL CONTENTS

?   two nickels   ?

10¢

We know that in the remaining two boxes, A and C, there are three nickels (15¢) and four nickels (20¢) in some order. This implies two possible scenarios:

Scenario 1

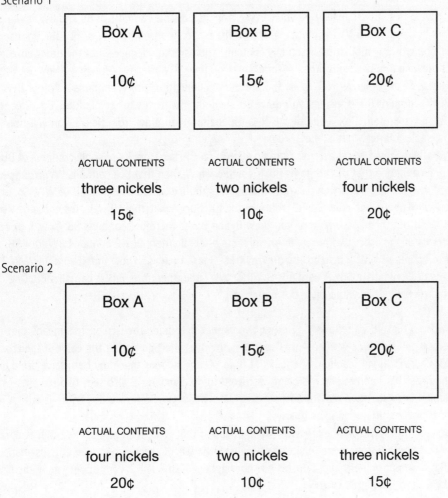

| Box A | Box B | Box C |
| 10¢ | 15¢ | 20¢ |

ACTUAL CONTENTS	ACTUAL CONTENTS	ACTUAL CONTENTS
three nickels	two nickels	four nickels
15¢	10¢	20¢

Scenario 2

| Box A | Box B | Box C |
| 10¢ | 15¢ | 20¢ |

ACTUAL CONTENTS	ACTUAL CONTENTS	ACTUAL CONTENTS
four nickels	two nickels	three nickels
20¢	10¢	15¢

In Scenario 1, C is labeled correctly as containing 20¢, which is contrary to the given fact that it is labeled incorrectly. Thus, we reject this scenario. Scenario 2, on the other hand, produces no contradictions: A contains 20¢, B contains 10¢ and C contains 15¢.

49. The actual contents of each box can be determined in just one drawing if that drawing is made from Box C.

Try drawing an item from Box A. As you can see from its possible contents of BW and WW, if you draw a B, then Box A contains BW. If you draw a W, then the box contains either BW or WW, and your second draw will tell you which combination it actually contains. You can then determine the actual contents of the other two boxes without drawing any ties from them. Assume that you got BW in two draws. Now look at the possible contents of Boxes B and C. By the process of elimination, Box B contains BB (not BW) and, therefore, Box C contains WW. If instead you drew WW, then, by the process of elimination, Box C contains BB (not WW) and, therefore, Box B contains BW. So, if you draw from Box A, you will need two drawings to be able to infer what is in each box.

Let's try drawing from Box B instead. As you can see from its possible contents of BB and BW, if you draw a W, then that box contains BW. If you draw a B, then the box contains either BW or BB, and your second draw will tell you which combination it actually contains. You can then deduce what the other boxes contain without drawing any ties from them. Assume that you have BW after two drawings. Now, look at the possible contents of the other two boxes. By the process of elimination, Box A contains WW (not BW) and, therefore, Box C contains BB. If instead you drew BB, then, by the process of elimination, Box C contains WW (not BB) and, therefore, Box A contains BW. Once again, if you draw from Box B, you will need two drawings to be able to infer what is in each box.

Let's see what happens if you draw first from Box C. As you can see from its possible contents of BB and WW, if you draw a B, then that box contains BB. If you draw a W, then that box contains WW. Your second draw is therefore unnecessary, since you know that it will produce a match—either BB or WW. So, in one drawing, you will know what is in Box C. You can then deduce what the other boxes contain without drawing any ties from them. Assume that you drew B, and Box C therefore contains BB. Now, look at the possible contents of the other two boxes. By the process of elimination, Box B contains BW (not BB) and, therefore, Box A contains WW. If instead you drew W from Box C, then you know that it contains WW. Then, by the process of elimination, Box A contains BW (not WW) and, therefore, Box B contains BB. One draw will allow you to reason this whole thing out correctly.

50. One of the women reasons as follows: The other two cannot determine their color. This means that I too have a red cross. Call the three women A, B, C, and A is the one who figured out the color of the cross on her head. Consider A's initial reaction. She looks at B and C and notices that they both have a red cross. Naturally, she raises her hand as she has been instructed to do. Similarly, B also sees two red crosses and raises her hand. C also sees two red crosses; she too raises her hand. So how did A figure it out? A must have had a flash of insight, thinking as follows:

"Let me assume that I have a blue cross on my forehead. If that is so, then one of the other two, say B, would know that she doesn't have a blue cross because otherwise C, seeing two blue crosses—mine and B's—would not have put up her hand. But this has not happened, so B and C cannot determine their color. This means that I too have a red cross."

CHAPTER 5

1. The bull weighs 1,000 pounds, whether it stands on four legs or on three. If you do not see this, perform the following analogous experiment. Stand on a scale and look at the weight that the scale shows. Then, staying on the scale, lift up one of your feet. Has your weight changed? It hasn't.

2. $6.20 (one dollar per consonant, five cents per vowel)

3. If one of the coins is not the nickel, then the other one is. The brother has a dime and nickel.

4. Five minutes. You would not boil five eggs separately, one after the other. If you did, you would need five minutes to boil the first egg, then another five minutes to boil the second egg, and so on. But, whether you boil one, two, five or a million eggs at one time, it takes only five minutes.

5. A man who leaves a widow is a dead man, and a dead man cannot marry his widow's sister.

6. Twelve. A dozen is a dozen, no matter what the stamps cost.

7. The trap in this puzzle is not to be found in any single word, but in the way in which the numerical facts are laid out. The manager kept $25 of the $30 he was given. The women got back $3 ($1 each). This adds up to $25 + $3 = $28. The remaining $2 were pocketed by the bellhop. There is no missing dollar.

8. Since one hour is equal to sixty minutes, then one hour and twenty minutes is equal to eighty minutes. There is nothing to explain, because it took the reaction one hour and twenty minutes or, in equivalent terms, eighty minutes to occur, no matter what the chemist was wearing.

9. If this puzzle stumped you, it is because you interpreted 1994 and 1984 as representing calendar years. Instead, they should be interpreted literally as digits: one thousand nine hundred and ninety-four dollar bills ($1,994) are worth more than one thousand nine hundred and eighty-four dollars ($1,984).

10. Shadows have no hue—they are all the same.

11. Once, because 25 − 1 = 24. If you subtract one again, it would be from twenty-four (24 − 1 = 23), and so on.

12. Eight. The one boy the farmer had was a brother to all seven sisters. The seven sisters did have a brother—the same one.

13. Like puzzle 7, the deception here is not to be found in any specific word, but in the layout of the numerical facts. Here's how they should have been laid out to avoid the apparent discrepancy. First, the bookstore salesclerk received nothing for the $3 book, since the counterfeit $10 bill was worth nothing. From the outset, he was out $3. That $3 went to the customer. Now, consider what happened in the other transaction, the one between the bookstore and record-store salesclerks. The bookstore salesclerk received ten genuine $1 bills from his record-store colleague. Thus, at first, the record-store salesclerk was out $10. When the bookstore salesclerk got back to his store, he gave $7 of the ten good bills to the customer and put the remaining good $3 in his pocket. The end result of this transaction was that the bookstore salesclerk was out another $7, while the customer gained $7. Altogether, the customer gained $10, a $3 book and $7 in good bills. That ends the bookstore salesclerk's transaction with the customer. At this point, the book salesclerk was out the $3 for the book, not the $7 that he gave back as change to the customer, as that came out of the pocket of the record-store salesclerk. When the record-store salesclerk asked for her $10 back, the bookstore salesclerk still had the $3 in his pocket left over from the $10 she had given him previously. So he gave her back her $3 and made up the $7 difference from his own pocket. In total, therefore, the bookstore salesclerk was out the $3 book and the $7 from his pocket, or $10 in total.

14. According to Carroll, the clock that doesn't run at all keeps the best time, depending on what one means by best time. At 12:00 midnight of the first day, the two clocks are synchronized. After that first day, the clock that loses one minute per day will be off by one minute at midnight, showing 11:59. After the second day, it will be off by two minutes at midnight, showing 11:58. And so on. After the sixtieth day, it will be off by one hour at midnight, showing 11:00. The clock will have to lose twelve hours to become synchronized once again with the stopped clock—that is, to show 12:00 correctly. Since it takes sixty days for every hour it loses, it will need 720 days ($60 \times 12 = 720$) to become synchronized again. That is almost two years. The stopped clock, on the other hand, shows 12:00 correctly twice a day—at noon and at midnight.

15. No matter how many times one tries to draw four straight lines without lifting the pencil, a dot is always left over—if you keep the lines within the square. It is at this point where insight thinking comes into play: "What would happen if I extend one or more of the four lines beyond the box?" That hunch turns out, in fact, to be the relevant insight. One possible solution is shown.

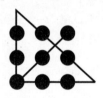

16. Six lines are required. Below is one possible solution. There are others.

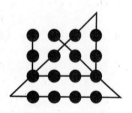

17. Eight. One possible solution is shown.

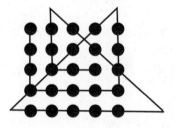

18. This puzzle seems to be unsolvable. How-ever, the puzzle does not prohibit us from putting one cup inside another. By doing so, the same set of coins can belong to more than one cup. Put the ten coins into the three cups separately as shown.

Now, insert the cup with two coins inside it into the cup with one coin inside it. There is no empty cup, and there are seven coins in one cup and three in another.

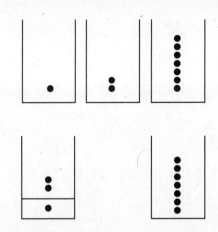

19. Borrow another camel to make eighteen and divide up the eighteen camels according to the required pro-portions. One-half of eighteen is nine; one-third of eighteen is six; and one-ninth of eighteen is two. Add these up: 9 + 6 + 2 = 17. You can now give the eighteenth camel back.

20. The puzzle does not say that all the oranges were taken out of the box. My sister left one of the oranges in the box, instead of taking it out, and gave it (along with the box) to one of her friends.

21. In addition, the sum of leftovers (the right-column figures) does not equal the sum of the amounts sub-tracted (the left-column figures). The column on the left side contains the actual dollars that the brother took out. These add up, as they should, to $50. But the figures in the column on the right side are leftovers. When the brother took out $20, he had $50 − $20 = $30 left over; when he took out the next $15, he had $30 − $15 = $15 left over and so on. There is no reason for these leftovers to add up to $50.

22. Twenty times: 4, 14, 24, 34, 40, 41, 42, 43, 44 (twice!), 45, 46, 47, 48, 49, 54, 64, 74, 84, 94

23. Wet feet

24. It is better to write it on paper or using some electronic device.

25. Get help.

26. The letters *H, F, K, N, Y* and *Z* all consist of three straight lines.

27. Get a ladder or a stool that is high enough or ask a very tall friend.

28. Stand the sign back up and take a look. It might help.

29. Jack was an infant who was taken to the doctor for a regular check-up.

30. You can make the digit 4 with three lines.

31. $5 + \dfrac{5}{5} = 6$

32. $9 + \dfrac{9}{9} + \dfrac{9}{9} + \dfrac{9}{9} = 12$

33. $9 + \sqrt{9} = 12$ (because $\sqrt{9} = 3$)

34. $\sqrt{9} = 3$

35. $1 - \dfrac{1}{1} = 0$, or $(1 \times 1) - 1 = 0$, or $\dfrac{1}{1} - 1 = 0$

36. $2 - \dfrac{2}{2} + \dfrac{2}{2} = 2$

37. III + II = V *(The puzzle refers to Roman numerals.)*

38. 100

39. $9 \times 0 = 0$

40. IV *(This is the Roman numeral for four.)*

41. $2 - 2 + \dfrac{2}{2} = 1$ *(There are other possibilities.)*

42. $2 \div \dfrac{2}{2} = 2$ or $\dfrac{(2 \times 2)}{2} = 2$

43. $\sqrt{49} = 7$

44. one *(These three letters spell the word for 1.)*

45. The twenty-eighth day. The snake gains 1 foot per day. At the end of the first day, it has gone up 3 feet and fallen 2 feet. So, if we were to calibrate the well like a number line, the snake would end up at level one above bottom. At the beginning of the second day, it starts from level one, goes up 3 feet, and slides back 2 feet, ending up at level two above ground. At the beginning of the third day, it starts at level two, and so on. Project to the beginning of day twenty-eight, when the snake starts from level twenty-seven. Here's the twist. When it goes up 3 feet on that day, it reaches the top (since the well is 30 feet deep) and simply slides out.

46. Forty days. Since my dad smoked only two-thirds of a cigarette, he therefore would leave a butt equal to one-third of a cigarette. For every three cigarettes smoked, he was able to piece together a new cigarette (one-third butt + one-third butt + one-third butt = one new cigarette). After smoking the original twenty-seven cigarettes, he was thus able to make nine new cigarettes from the butts. If you stopped here, simply adding twenty-seven (the number of cigarettes my dad smoked originally) to nine (the number of new cigarettes made and smoked), you would come up with thirty-six (total number of cigarettes smoked by my dad). But the nine new cigarettes also produced butts, and from these nine butts, my dad was able to make three more cigarettes (three butts = one new cigarette). But, those three extra cigarettes produced three butts of their own, yielding yet one more cigarette. Altogether, therefore, my dad smoked 27 + 9 + 3 + 1 = 40 cigarettes before giving up his bad habit. That took forty days.

47. Fifteen miles. The bike riders were twenty miles apart. They both traveled at ten mph. After one hour, each had covered a distance of ten miles. That's the midpoint between them and, thus, their meeting point. The fly flew back and forth for one hour at fifteen mph. Thus, in that hour it flew 15 miles. End of matter. The reason why this puzzle gives many solvers difficulties is because the fly's distance is described in terms of a back-and-forth movement. The fly will cover a certain distance, not a certain direction, within the specified period of one hour. It doesn't matter if that distance can be mapped out as a straight line or as a back-and-forth movement.

48. It helps enormously in solving this classic puzzle if you see the books as they line up on a bookshelf. We are told that the bookworm started on the first page of the first book to the left (Vol. I). Think carefully! If you were to pick up Vol. I, where would the first page of that volume be? It would be on the right end of Vol. I, as you look at Vol. I on the bookshelf! If you do not quite see this, take three books, line them up as shown and check out where the first page of the first book to the left is.

The bookworm stopped at the last page of the last book to the right (Vol. III). Where is the last page of Vol. III? It is on the left end of Vol. III as you look at that volume on the bookshelf. Once again, if you have difficulty seeing this, just line three books up as shown and then check out for yourself where the last page of the book to the right is.

Now you calculate the distance the bookworm covered. The bookworm started on page 1 of Vol. I, as shown in the diagram, went through its front cover ($\frac{1}{2}$ inch), through the back cover of Vol. II ($\frac{1}{2}$ inch), through the pages of Vol. II (2 inches), then through the front cover of Vol. II ($\frac{1}{2}$ inch), and finally through the back cover of Vol. III ($\frac{1}{2}$ inch), at which point it reached the last page of Vol. III. As you can see, the bookworm went through a distance of $\frac{1}{2} + \frac{1}{2} + 2 + \frac{1}{2} + \frac{1}{2} = 4$ inches. The bookworm traveled a total of 4 inches from the front page of Vol. I to the last page of Vol. III.

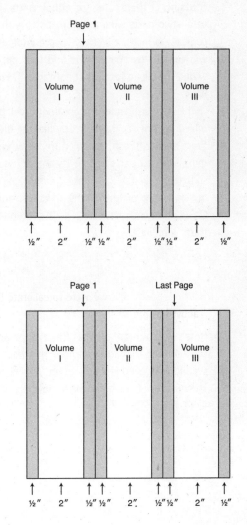

49. One-third wine. The puzzle tells us that container A is half full with wine and that container B, which is twice the size of A, is one-quarter full with wine. First, draw the two containers, making B twice the size of A. When you fill half of A and one-quarter B with wine, the containers will look like this:

Notice that there is, in fact, the same amount of wine in the two containers. This is due to their different sizes. Now fill the containers with water.

As you can see, A has two equal portions of wine and water, while B has three parts water and one part wine. Between the two containers, there are six equal parts in total—two parts wine and four parts water. Logically, a mixture of these two containers will contain two parts wine and four parts water. That is, in fact, what container C will have.

The wine and water in container C will be mixed up, not separated neatly like the diagram above. But in that mixture, wine will make up two parts out of its six, or two-sixths, and water will make up four parts out of its six, or four-sixths. In conclusion, C's mixture will have two-sixths, or one-third, wine in it.

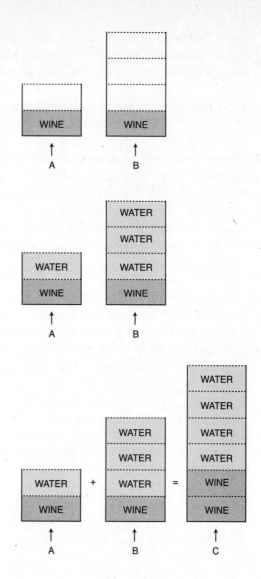

50. Here's a paraphrase of what Gauss apparently said. There are forty-nine pairs of numbers between one and one hundred that add up to one hundred. This can be seen by adding them in pairs—first with second last, second with third last and so on: 1 + 99 = 100, 2 + 98 = 100, 3 + 97 = 100 and so on. That makes 4,900. The number 50, being in the middle, stands alone, as does 100, standing at the end. Adding 50 and 100 to 4,900 gives 5,050.

CHAPTER 6

1.

5	4	3	2	1
4	3	1	5	2
3	1	2	4	5
2	5	4	1	3
1	2	5	3	4

2.

1	4	5	3	2
3	2	1	5	4
4	5	3	2	1
5	1	2	4	3
2	3	4	1	5

3.

5	2	1	3	4
3	4	2	1	5
4	1	3	5	2
1	5	4	2	3
2	3	5	4	1

4.

1	3	5	2	4
5	2	4	1	3
4	1	3	5	2
3	5	2	4	1
2	4	1	3	5

5.

6	5	4	3	2	1
5	3	1	6	4	2
4	6	2	5	1	3
3	1	5	2	6	4
2	4	6	1	3	5
1	2	3	4	5	6

6.

6	3	2	5	4	1
5	4	6	1	2	3
4	6	1	2	3	5
3	5	4	6	1	2
2	1	5	3	6	4
1	2	3	4	5	6

7.

1	6	7	4	3	5	2
4	1	3	5	6	2	7
7	2	5	6	4	1	3
6	5	4	7	2	3	1
2	7	1	3	5	6	4
3	4	6	2	1	7	5
5	3	2	1	7	4	6

8.

1	2	5	3	4	7	6
2	4	1	7	6	5	3
3	5	7	6	1	4	2
4	6	2	5	3	1	7
5	7	3	1	2	6	4
6	1	4	2	7	3	5
7	3	6	4	5	2	1

9.

8	4	5	3	1	2	9	7	6
2	9	7	6	8	5	1	3	4
1	3	6	7	4	9	8	5	2
6	8	3	4	9	1	7	2	5
4	5	9	2	7	8	6	1	3
7	2	1	5	6	3	4	8	9
9	7	2	8	3	6	5	4	1
5	1	8	9	2	4	3	6	7
3	6	4	1	5	7	2	9	8

10.

8	9	4	1	7	6	5	2	3
3	5	6	2	9	8	7	4	1
2	1	7	3	4	5	8	6	9
6	7	9	5	1	2	3	8	4
5	8	2	4	3	9	1	7	6
1	4	3	6	8	7	9	5	2
9	3	5	7	2	4	6	1	8
7	2	1	8	6	3	4	9	5
4	6	8	9	5	1	2	3	7

11.

1	2	3	4
3	4	2	1
4	3	1	2
2	1	4	3

12.

3	2	1	4
4	1	2	3
2	3	4	1
1	4	3	2

13.

1	3	4	2
2	4	3	1
4	2	1	3
3	1	2	4

14.

3	4	1	2
2	1	4	3
4	2	3	1
1	3	2	4

15.

1	4	2	3
3	2	4	1
2	1	3	4
4	3	1	2

16.

4	3	1	2
1	2	3	4
3	4	2	1
2	1	4	3

17.

1	2	3	4	5	6
4	5	6	1	2	3
3	4	1	2	6	5
5	6	2	3	4	1
2	3	5	6	1	4
6	1	4	5	3	2

18.

2	1	3	5	6	4
4	5	6	2	3	1
1	3	2	6	4	5
6	4	5	3	1	2
5	6	4	1	2	3
3	2	1	4	5	6

19.

6	5	1	4	2	3
4	2	3	5	6	1
3	4	5	6	1	2
2	1	6	3	4	5
5	6	2	1	3	4
1	3	4	2	5	6

20.

3	6	1	5	2	4
4	5	2	6	1	3
6	2	3	1	4	5
5	1	4	2	3	6
2	3	5	4	6	1
1	4	6	3	5	2

21.

4	3	1	7	9	6	2	5	8
5	7	9	3	8	2	6	1	4
2	8	6	1	5	4	9	3	7
7	2	3	4	6	5	8	9	1
1	5	8	9	2	3	4	7	6
9	6	4	8	1	7	3	2	5
6	4	7	5	3	9	1	8	2
8	9	5	2	4	1	7	6	3
3	1	2	6	7	8	5	4	9

22.

3	2	7	9	6	5	8	1	4
6	1	8	2	7	4	3	5	9
9	5	4	1	8	3	7	2	6
1	9	6	4	3	2	5	8	7
5	4	3	8	1	7	9	6	2
7	8	2	5	9	6	1	4	3
8	7	5	6	4	9	2	3	1
2	6	9	3	5	1	4	7	8
4	3	1	7	2	8	6	9	5

23.

9	4	7	2	6	8	1	5	3
8	1	5	4	3	7	6	2	9
2	6	3	9	5	1	4	8	7
1	3	2	7	8	4	5	9	6
6	5	4	3	9	2	8	7	1
7	8	9	6	1	5	2	3	4
3	9	1	5	2	6	7	4	8
5	7	8	1	4	3	9	6	2
4	2	6	8	7	9	3	1	5

24.

6	5	7	8	2	3	1	4	9
9	8	1	7	4	5	2	3	6
4	2	3	1	9	6	8	7	5
2	3	5	4	7	9	6	1	8
7	1	4	2	6	8	5	9	3
8	6	9	3	5	1	4	2	7
1	4	6	5	3	7	9	8	2
3	9	8	6	1	2	7	5	4
5	7	2	9	8	4	3	6	1

25.

6	1	8	7	4	5	9	3	2
4	7	3	6	2	9	1	5	8
2	9	5	3	1	8	4	7	6
1	5	7	9	3	6	8	2	4
9	2	4	8	5	1	3	6	7
3	8	6	2	7	4	5	9	1
5	6	2	1	8	3	7	4	9
7	4	1	5	9	2	6	8	3
8	3	9	4	6	7	2	1	5

26.

9	3	5	8	4	1	2	7	6
7	6	4	2	9	5	3	1	8
2	1	8	3	6	7	4	9	5
5	2	6	1	7	8	9	3	4
8	9	3	6	2	4	1	5	7
1	4	7	5	3	9	6	8	2
3	5	2	9	8	6	7	4	1
6	7	1	4	5	3	8	2	9
4	8	9	7	1	2	5	6	3

27.

9	3	2	4	7	5	1	8	6
5	8	1	3	6	9	7	2	4
6	4	7	1	2	8	3	5	9
2	1	5	9	4	7	6	3	8
3	6	9	5	8	2	4	7	1
8	7	4	6	3	1	5	9	2
7	2	6	8	1	3	9	4	5
4	5	3	2	9	6	8	1	7
1	9	8	7	5	4	2	6	3

28.

2	4	5	9	3	7	6	1	8
3	1	7	2	6	8	9	5	4
9	8	6	1	4	5	3	2	7
7	5	1	6	2	4	8	3	9
6	3	2	8	7	9	5	4	1
4	9	8	5	1	3	7	6	2
8	2	3	4	9	6	1	7	5
5	7	4	3	8	1	2	9	6
1	6	9	7	5	2	4	8	3

29.

7	9	6	3	4	1	2	5	8
5	2	4	9	7	8	6	1	3
1	8	3	6	2	5	7	9	4
8	3	1	7	9	2	5	4	6
6	4	5	1	8	3	9	2	7
2	7	9	5	6	4	3	8	1
3	1	2	4	5	7	8	6	9
9	5	7	8	1	6	4	3	2
4	6	8	2	3	9	1	7	5

30.

3	6	5	9	8	1	4	2	7
2	1	4	5	6	7	9	8	3
9	7	8	4	2	3	1	5	6
6	8	7	1	5	4	2	3	9
5	3	2	6	9	8	7	1	4
4	9	1	7	3	2	8	6	5
7	4	6	2	1	5	3	9	8
8	2	9	3	4	6	5	7	1
1	5	3	8	7	9	6	4	2

31.

E	A	B	I	D	G	C	H	F
G	H	D	F	E	C	A	B	I
C	F	I	H	A	B	E	G	D
A	D	C	B	I	F	H	E	G
H	B	E	G	C	D	I	F	A
I	G	F	A	H	E	D	C	B
D	E	G	C	F	A	B	I	H
B	C	H	D	G	I	F	A	E
F	I	A	E	B	H	G	D	C

32.

A	I	B	F	H	C	D	G	E
H	C	G	E	D	I	F	A	B
E	F	D	G	B	A	H	I	C
I	H	E	A	C	B	G	F	D
B	G	A	D	E	F	C	H	I
F	D	C	H	I	G	E	B	A
C	A	H	I	G	E	B	D	F
G	E	I	B	F	D	A	C	H
D	B	F	C	A	H	I	E	G

33.

I	E	A	B	F	D	C	H	G
D	G	H	A	I	C	E	B	F
C	B	F	E	H	G	D	I	A
F	C	E	G	B	I	H	A	D
H	I	D	F	E	A	G	C	B
B	A	G	C	D	H	F	E	I
G	H	I	D	C	B	A	F	E
A	F	B	H	G	E	I	D	C
E	D	C	I	A	F	B	G	H

34.

E	D	I	C	H	G	B	F	A
A	C	B	F	E	D	H	G	I
F	H	G	A	B	I	D	C	E
B	I	F	D	C	H	A	E	G
C	A	H	B	G	E	I	D	F
D	G	E	I	F	A	C	H	B
H	E	A	G	I	C	F	B	D
I	F	C	E	D	B	G	A	H
G	B	D	H	A	F	E	I	C

35.

4	1	2	7	14
3	2	1	4	10
5	6	3	8	22
1	2	1	2	6
13	11	7	21	

36.

1	1	1	2	5
3	9	6	7	25
5	1	1	2	9
2	1	8	1	12
11	12	16	12	

37.

2	3	5	6	16
1	9	9	5	24
8	5	2	1	16
9	6	1	2	18
20	23	17	14	

38.

9	9	8	8	34
6	6	5	9	26
5	5	5	3	18
1	1	1	2	5
21	21	19	22	

39.

7	8	5	1	21
7	8	9	1	25
7	2	8	1	18
1	1	1	1	4
22	19	23	4	

40.

4	4	4	4	16
7	7	4	1	19
1	2	4	1	8
1	1	4	5	11
13	14	16	11	

41.

1	6	3	1	11
9	1	1	2	13
8	5	3	3	19
7	4	1	4	16
25	16	8	10	

42.

4	5	4	1	14
9	8	8	9	34
1	1	2	2	6
7	6	5	1	19
21	20	19	13	

43. Rows are products, columns are sums.

2	2	1	1	4
3	3	3	2	54
1	7	2	2	28
5	2	1	5	50
11	14	7	10	

44. Columns are products, rows are sums.

2	1	3	1	7
2	5	3	4	14
1	2	1	2	6
2	8	1	6	17
8	80	9	48	

In the puzzles below, the product-producing rows and columns are the highlighted ones. The other rows and columns are the sum-producing ones.

45.

1	1	3	1	5	15
1	5	5	2	1	14
1	5	1	4	1	12
1	3	6	2	1	36
1	1	1	1	2	6
5	15	16	10	10	

46.

9	2	3	1	1	54
2	9	9	9	9	38
1	9	5	6	4	25
1	1	5	5	2	50
2	1	1	1	1	6
36	22	23	22	17	

47.

2	9	1	2	1	15
2	2	2	2	3	48
2	8	5	2	3	20
2	1	2	2	3	24
3	1	1	1	3	9
11	21	20	9	81	

48.

4	1	1	2	4	32
4	8	1	3	3	19
1	8	7	1	2	19
1	8	7	5	2	23
4	8	7	1	1	21
64	33	23	30	48	

49.

1	1	1	1	1	2	2
1	6	1	9	3	4	24
5	2	1	1	1	5	50
5	6	1	9	1	1	23
5	1	5	1	1	1	25
5	2	5	9	1	8	30
22	18	14	30	8	21	

50.

9	1	3	2	5	6	26
9	1	3	2	4	2	21
9	1	3	1	2	1	54
9	3	3	1	4	5	25
9	1	3	1	1	1	27
8	1	3	6	9	1	28
53	3	18	24	25	16	

CHAPTER 7

1. The magic constant is 15.

8	1	6
3	5	7
4	9	2

For this first puzzle only, we will go over the additions.

ROWS	COLUMNS	DIAGONALS
8 + 1 + 6 = 15	8 + 3 + 4 = 15	8 + 5 + 2 = 15
3 + 5 + 7 = 15	1 + 5 + 9 = 15	6 + 5 + 4 = 15
4 + 9 + 2 = 15	6 + 7 + 2 = 15	

2.

4	9	2
3	5	7
8	1	6

3.

8	3	4
1	5	9
6	7	2

4. The magic constant is 30.

16	2	12
6	10	14
8	18	4

5. The magic constant is 27.

15	1	11
5	9	13
7	17	3

6. The magic constant is 36.

15	10	11
8	12	16
13	14	9

7.

67	1	43
13	37	61
31	73	7

8. The magic constant is 9d.

2½d	5d	1½d
2d	3d	4d
4½d	1d	3½d

9. The magic constant is 34.

16	3	2	13
5	10	11	8
9	6	7	12
4	15	14	1

10.

3	71	5	23
53	11	37	1
17	13	41	31
29	7	19	47

11. 19. The numbers increase by three.

12. 6. The difference between each consecutive pair of numbers, starting with the first two, is 1: 4 − 3 = 1, 5 − 4 = 1 and so on.

13. 128. Each number is twice the one before it.

14. 23. Each number in the sequence is a consecutive prime number.

15. 55. Starting with 2, each number is the sum of the previous two.

16. 44. Starting with 4, every number is the sum of the previous three.

17. 2,187. The numbers are in ascending powers of 3: $3^1 = 3$, $3^2 = 9$ and so on.

18. 7. The numbers are in descending powers of 7: $16,807 = 7^5$; $2,401 = 7^4$ and so on.

19. 49. Each number is a square of the numbers in sequence: $1 = 1^2$, $4 = 2^2$, $9 = 3^2$, $16 = 4^2$ and so on.

20. 48. Add the first two numbers and subtract 1 from the sum (3 + 2 = 5 − 1 = 4). Then add the new number to the previous one and subtract 1 (4 + 2 = 6 − 1 = 5): and so on).

21. 96. There are several ways to explain the built-in pattern in the sequence. Here's one. There are two alternating sequences. In the first one, the numbers in sequence (1, 2, 3, 4, . . .) occur in every odd spot; in the second, the numbers in reverse sequence, starting with 100, occur in every even spot (100, 99, 98, 97, . . .).

22. 32. There are two alternating sequences: one increasing by powers of 2 and the other by powers of 5. In exponent form, the sequence looks like this: 2^1, 5^1, 2^2, 5^2, 2^3, 5^3, 2^4 and so on.

23. 8. Two odd numbers in sequence are followed by an even number in sequence: 1, 3, 2, followed by the next two odd numbers, 5 and 7, and then the second even number 4 and so on.

24. 354. The sequence consists of a number followed by its palindrome, or number with the digits in reverse.

25. 5. Starting with the first number, every third number is followed by two numbers that, when added together, produce it: 4 = 2 + 2, 6 = 3 + 3, 8 = 5 + 3 and so on.

26. 8. Starting with 3, every next (or alternate) number is produced by adding the two digits of the preceding number: 3 = 1 + 2, 6 = 2 + 4 and so on.

27. 1. Starting with the first 1, every next (or alternate) number is produced by subtracting the two digits of the preceding number: 1 = 2 − 1, 2 = 4 − 2 and so on.

28. We will go through the reasoning involved in solving the first cryptarithm only, since the same kind of reasoning is involved in solving all cryptarithms. Look at the right-most column. There is only one digit that, when added to 2, produces 4 in that column, and that is 2. Let's put it in its proper spot.

```
    *   2
+   5   2
─────────
*   0   4
```

Next, consider the number to be put under the plus sign. One is the only number that can possibly carry over in that position when the two digits in the previous column are added together—even if the column has itself a carryover from the column before, which, in this case, it does not. If you do not see this, consider the column in question. There are ten digits, including zero. The maximum that two different digits can add up to is 17, which would occur with the two largest digits, 9 and 8. Even if there were a carryover from the previous column, the maximum 9 + 8 + 1 (carryover) could possibly add up to is 18.

```
    *   2
+   5   2
─────────
1   0   4
```

Look at the remaining column, which already has 5 in it. Only one number, when added to 5, produces 0 and a carryover—another 5, as 5 + 5 = 10. That completes the reconstruction.

```
    5   2
+   5   2
─────────
1   0   4
```

29.

```
      8  8  2  1
   +  9  2  0  1
   ─────────────
   1  8  0  2  2
```

30.

```
      3  5  8
   −     5  9
   ────────────
         2  9  9
```

31.

```
      2  3  4
   −  1  9  0
   ───────────
            4  4
```

32.

```
      2  8
   x     8
   ─────────
      2  2  4
```

33.

```
      9  9  9
   x        9
   ───────────
   8  9  9  1
```

34.

```
         5  1  1
   x        1  5
   ──────────────
      2  5  5  5
      5  1  1
   ──────────────
      7  6  6  5
```

35. 45 + 98 − 3 = 140

36. 12 x 3 ÷ 4 = 9

37. 98 ÷ 2 ÷ 7 x 2 = 14

38. 2 + 34 + 12 ÷ 1 = 48

39. 15 + 21 ÷ 3 ÷ 4 = 3

40. 12 + 9 − 5 x 2 ÷ 8 = 4

41. We will go through the reasoning involved in solving the first puzzle only, since the same kind of reasoning (basic arithmatical deduction) is involved in solving all alphametics. It can instantly be established, as in puzzle 28, that the letter t under the plus sign is a carryover digit equal to 1, because 1 is the only number possible in that position in a layout when the two digits in the previous column are added together (in this case n + t) even if the column has itself a carryover from the column before. If you still do not understand this, consider the column in question. There are ten digits, including zero. The maximum that two different digits can add up to is 17, which would occur with the two largest digits, 9 and 8. Let the two digits in the column equal 9 and 8, just for the sake of illustration.

```
    9  o
+   8  o
─────────
1   7  n
```

Do you see that t can only equal 1? Even if there were a carryover from the previous column, the maximum 9 + 8 + 1 (carryover) could possibly add up to is 18. Having deduced that t = 1, we can put its numerical value in the layout, noticing that it occurs in two places:

```
    n  o
+   1  o
─────────
1   e  n
```

Next look at the n + 1 column. The addition of n + 1 produces a carryover. So, the n is either 8 or 9, since no other available numbers will do so. Let's try n = 9, noting that n occurs twice:

```
    9  o
+   1  o
─────────
1   e  9
```

This does not work out. Why? Look at the right-hand column. There are two same digits there, represented by the letter o, which, when added together, should equal 9. There are no such digits—try it if you don't believe me. Thus, the only possible number that n can be is 8:

```
    8  o
+   1  o
─────────
1   e  8
```

Now, look at the 8 + 1 = e column. The letter e can be either 9 or 0 (with a carryover from the previous column). It cannot be 9, because then there would be no carryover (under the plus sign). So, it must be 0:

```
    8  o
+   1  o
─────────
1   0  8
```

This means that the o + o = 8 in the right-hand column must produce a carryover. And the only two digits that will generate this result are 9 + 9 = 18. We have now solved the alphametic, as you can see:

```
    8  9
+   1  9
─────────
1   0  8
```

42.

```
    9  0  9
 +  8  0  8
 ──────────
 1  7  1  7
```

43.

```
       2  1  2
 x        1  2
 ─────────────
       4  2  4
    2  1  2
 ─────────────
    2  5  4  4
```

44.

```
    9  5  6  7
 +  1  0  8  5
 ──────────────
 1  0  6  5  2
```

45. Fifty-nine ties. Counting ties by ones, twos, threes and so on is the equivalent of dividing the ties into smaller groups of one tie, two ties, three ties and so on. To solve this puzzle, you must identify the number of ties between fifty and sixty, which, when divided by three, gives a remainder of two—a remainder of two is equivalent to saying that there are two ties left over—and when divided by five, gives a remainder of four. First, divide the numbers between fifty and sixty by three, identifying those that leave a remainder of two. If you do so correctly, you will get the following divisions that produce a remainder of two:

$50 \div 3 = 16$, remainder $= 2$
$53 \div 3 = 17$, remainder $= 2$
$56 \div 3 = 18$, remainder $= 2$
$59 \div 3 = 19$, remainder $= 2$

Now, proceed to determine what number will leave a remainder of four when it is divided by five.

$59 \div 5 = 11$, remainder $= 4$

Thus, fifty-nine ties is the answer. And, in fact, when you count fifty-nine ties three at a time, you'll get two left over; when you count them five at a time, you'll get four left over.

46. The eraser costs 2½¢. Here's how to reason. The pencil costs 50¢ *more* than what the eraser costs. Consider a few concrete examples: if the eraser costs 1¢, then the pencil will cost 1¢ + 50¢ *more* (= 51¢); if the eraser costs 2¢, then the pencil will cost 2¢ + 50¢ more (= 52)¢ and so on. The only price of the eraser that works, therefore, is 2½¢. Thus, the pencil costs 52½¢. Together, they do indeed add up to 55¢: 2½ + 52½ = 55.

47. 132 seconds. We know that at eight o'clock the clock makes eight strikes, taking seven seconds. Each interval between the strikes is one second long. This pattern applies to every hour on the hour. For example, at nine o'clock, the clock will make nine strikes, separated by eight intervals lasting one second each, so it will take the clock eight seconds to strike nine o'clock. And so on. In general, at each hour the clock will need one second less than the number of the hour to strike that hour. The one exception is one o'clock, when the strike coincides with the hour and thus requires zero seconds. The following chart is a good way to organize the progression.

HOUR	STRIKES	TIME TAKEN
1:00	1	0 sec. *(The strike coincides with the hour.)*
2:00	2	1 sec.
3:00	3	2 sec.
...	...	...
12:00	12	11 sec.

To find out how many seconds the clock has been striking from 1:00 to 12:00, all you have to do is add up the numbers in the *Time Taken* column. These are, as you can see, the first eleven numbers, starting with zero: 0 + 1 + 2 + 3 + 4 + 5 + 6 + 7 + 8 + 9 + 10 + 11 = 66 seconds. Since the clock goes around two times a day from 1:00 A.M. to 12:00 noon and from 1:00 P.M. to 12:00 midnight, the number of seconds the clock will be striking is twice this number: 66 x 2 = 132 seconds per day.

48. Saturday, June 5. Since Tuesday is June 1, then Monday, the day before, is May 31. Set up a time chart for the week of May 31. Gina (G) works every second day and Alexander (A) every third. As you can see, the two will be working together on Saturday, June 5.

	MONDAY	TUESDAY	WEDNESDAY	THURSDAY	FRIDAY	SATURDAY	SUNDAY
	May 31	June 1	June 2	June 3	June 4	June 5	June 6
Gina	G		G			G	
Alexander		A				A	

49. Saturday, October 13. As with puzzle 48, set up a time chart for the week of October 1, with *J* representing Jack and *S* representing Sarah.

	MONDAY	TUESDAY	WEDNESDAY	THURSDAY	FRIDAY	SATURDAY	SUNDAY
	October 1	October 2	October 3	October 4	October 5	October 6	October 7
Jack	J			J			J
Sarah						S	

Since they will apparently not be working together during that week, set up a chart for the week after. As you can see, their work schedules coincide on Saturday of that week.

	MONDAY	TUESDAY	WEDNESDAY	THURSDAY	FRIDAY	SATURDAY	SUNDAY
	October 8	October 9	October 10	October 11	October 12	October 13	October 14
Jack			J			J	
Sarah						S	

50. 18¢. My sister has two dimes, or 20¢. Four-fifths of 20¢ is 16¢. That amount (16¢) equals eight-ninths of what I have. Eight-ninths of 18¢ is 16¢, and so I have 18¢.

CHAPTER 8

1. Time. It flies, as in *Time flies*. It can be long and short, as in *It's been a long time* and *Time is short*. It can be put into a capsule, as in a *time capsule*.

2. Your name. Others use your name more than you do, even though it belongs to you.

3. A rainbow. The rainbow's colors are red, blue, purple and green, but no one can touch or even reach a rainbow.

4. Love. *Love is sweet, Love is bitter, Love blossoms* and *Love grows* are all common clichés about love.

5. Justice. The *scales of justice* and *justice is blind* are two common expressions about justice.

6. Fire. *Promethean, infernal* and *eternal* are all adjectives referring to fire.

7. Apple. The word *apple* appears in the expressions *golden apple* and the *apple of one's eye*. It is also known as the *forbidden fruit* (ever since the medieval interpretation of the biblical forbidden fruit as an apple).

8. Stink. Metaphorically speaking, you can *raise a stink*, and you can describe someone with money as *stinking rich*. Also, some jobs really *stink*, don't they?

9. The moon. A *honeymoon* and a *silvery moon* refer to love. And you've heard what happens when a *full moon* is out.

10. A smile. You can *wear a smile*, but someone who is angry with you might tell you to *take the smile off your face*.

11. (a) race, acre
(b) crate
(c) spot, tops, opts, post
(d) spit, pits
(e) lives, veils

12. (a) stripes
(b) spirited
(c) silent, enlist
(d) married
(e) tones, notes, seton *(surgical term referring to a skein of cotton)*

13. (a) spare mind
(b) pilots cheer or pilot's cheer
(c) dirty room
(d) the classroom
(e) a dog trail

14. (a) great help
(b) real fun
(c) best in prayer
(d) a stern sense
(e) I cry that sin

15. (a) conversation
(b) families
(c) butterfly
(d) software
(e) astronomers

16. (a) They see.
(b) a time to charm Venus
(c) built to stay free
(d) twelve plus one
(e) art's models

17. (a) I'm not as active.
(b) detect thieves
(c) elegant man
(d) bad credit
(e) Sit down, fearful lie!

18. (a) So, I'm cuter.
(b) genuine class
(c) screen is a storm
(d) He bugs Gore.
(e) a long darn era

19. (a) Nerd amid late TV
(b) and moan
(c) Do an angry hit.
(d) Won half the New World's glory.
(e) Governs a nice, quiet land.

20. (a) untied
(b) filled
(c) enormity
(d) fluster
(e) arch saints

21.

M	A	R	E	
D	R	E	A	M

22.

R	E	N	T	
T	R	E	N	D

23.

R	A	C	E	
C	R	A	N	E

24.

C	A	R	T		
T	R	A	C	E	
R	E	A	C	T	S

25.

C	A	P	E		
S	P	A	C	E	
P	L	A	C	E	S

26.

E	N	D	S		
N	E	R	D	S	
T	R	E	N	D	S

27.

A	C	E	S		
C	E	A	S	E	
C	R	E	A	S	E

28.

S	A	L	E			
L	E	A	S	E		
S	E	A	L	E	R	
P	L	E	A	S	E	R

29.

P	A	D	S			
S	P	A	D	E		
D	R	A	P	E	S	
P	A	R	A	D	E	S

30.

S	O	R	E			
P	O	R	E	S		
S	P	O	R	E	S	
R	E	P	O	S	E	S

31.

W	O	W
O	N	E
W	E	T

32.

L	O	T
O	U	R
T	R	Y

33.

T	R	A	P
R	A	R	E
A	R	T	S
P	E	S	T

34.

C	L	A	M
L	A	M	E
A	M	E	N
M	E	N	D

35.

P	A	C	K
A	B	L	E
C	L	U	E
K	E	E	P

36.

B	R	A	T
R	A	R	E
A	R	E	A
T	E	A	R

37.

M	A	K	E
A	R	I	D
K	I	T	E
E	D	E	N

38.

D	A	T	A
A	J	A	R
T	A	M	E
A	R	E	A

39.

S	A	I	L
A	C	R	E
I	R	I	S
L	E	S	S

40.

F	L	O	S	S
L	A	T	C	H
O	T	T	E	R
S	C	E	N	E
S	H	R	E	D

41. APE
APT
OPT
OAT
MAT
MAN

42. FLOUR
FLOOR
FLOOD
BLOOD
BROOD
BROAD
BREAD

43. SLEEP
BLEEP
BLEED
BREED
BREAD
DREAD
DREAM

44. ONE
OPE *(archaic for open)*
OPT
OUT
TUT *(clicking noise made with the tongue)*
TOT
TOO
TWO

45. BLACK
BLANK
BLINK
CLINK
CHINK
CHINE *(cut of meat)*
WHINE
WHITE

46. BLUE
GLUE
GLUT
GOUT
POUT
PORT
PART
PANT
PINT
PINK

47. RIVER
ROVER
COVER
COVES
CORES
CORNS
COINS
CHINS
SHINS
SHINE
SHONE
SHORE

48. WITCH
WINCH
WENCH
TENCH
TENTH
TENTS
TINTS
TILTS
TILLS
FILLS
FALLS
FAILS
FAIRS
FAIRY

49. HATE
HAVE (new letter)
HIVE (new letter)
LIVE (new letter)
VEIL (rearrangement)

50. IRON
ICON (new letter)
COIN (rearrangement)
CORN (new letter)
CORD (new letter)
LORD (new letter)
LOAD (new letter)
LEAD (new letter)

CHAPTER 9

1.

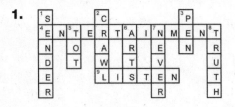

2.

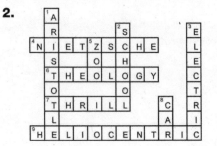

3.

4.

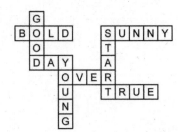

5.

6.

7.

8.

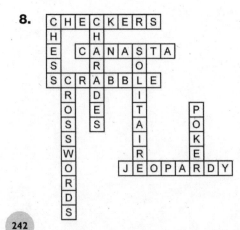

9.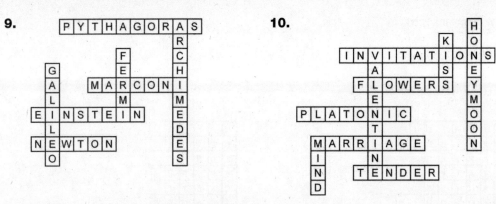

10.

11. Harrison Ford: *Star Wars, Raiders of the Lost Ark*

12. Madonna: *Desperately Seeking Susan, A League of Their Own*

13. Orson Welles: *Citizen Kane, Touch of Evil*

14. Sophia Loren: *Grumpier Old Men, Two Women*

15. Greta Garbo: *Mata Hari, Grand Hotel*

16. Jane Fonda: *Cat Ballou, The Morning After*

17. Tom Cruise: *Interview with the Vampire, Eyes Wide Shut*

18. Denzel Washington: *Malcolm X, The Bone Collector*

19. Whoopi Goldberg: *The Color Purple, Sister Act*

20. Meryl Streep: *The Deer Hunter, Music of the Heart*

21. Steven Spielberg: *Alien*

22. Alfred Hitchcock: *Seven*

23. Federico Fellini: *Death in Venice*

24. Stanley Kubrick: *History of Violence*

25. George Lucas: *The Fly*

26. Woody Allen: *The Odd Couple*

27. Jean-Luc Godard: *Spellbound*

28. Ingmar Bergman: *Open City*

29. Jodie Foster: *Enchanted*

30. Spike Lee: *Boyz N the Hood*

31.
1. VIVALDI
2. EXPLORER
3. NAPLES
4. ITALY
5. CANALS
6. ECONOMIC

32.
1. GREEK
2. REVOLT
3. EURO
4. EPIRUS
5. CRETE
6. EUROPE

33.
1. SHEEP
2. AFRICA
3. HOT
4. ARABIC
5. ROUTES
6. ALGERIA

34.
1. ASIA
2. FORESTS
3. RWANDA
4. ISLAM
5. COLONIAL
6. ANGOLA

35.
1. TRAVIATA
2. REQUIEM
3. RIGOLETTO
4. AIDA
5. ITALIAN

36.
1. HABAÑERA
2. SPAIN
3. PRIZE
4. CARMEN
5. CIGARETTE

37.
1. PAINTING
2. BUTTERFLY
3. TOSCA
4. LUCCA
5. VERDI
6. TURANDOT
7. ITALY

38.
1. WINTER
2. IOWA
3. SHOLES
4. CHEESE
5. OSHKOSH
6. NORTH
7. SUGAR
8. INDIANA
9. NORTHLAND

39.
1. SORBONNE
2. EIFFEL
3. ILE
4. NORMANDY
5. ENGLISH

40.
1. BASKETS
2. EMPEROR
3. IMPERIAL
4. JAPAN
5. INNER
6. NORTHERN
7. GREAT

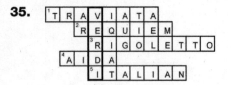

41.

D	A	N		B	R	O	W	N
1	2	3		4	5	6	7	3

42.

C	H	A	R	L	E	S		D	I	C	K	E	N	S
8	9	2	5	10	11	12		1	13	8	14	11	3	12

43.

V	I	R	G	I	N	I	A		W	O	O	L	F
15	13	5	16	13	3	13	2		7	6	6	10	17

44.

T	R	U	M	A	N		C	A	P	O	T	E
18	5	19	20	2	3		8	2	21	6	18	11

45.

L	E	O		T	O	L	S	T	O	Y
10	11	6		18	6	10	12	18	6	22

46.

A	N	N	E		R	I	C	E
2	3	3	11		5	13	8	11

47.

E	M	I	L	Y		D	I	C	K	I	N	S	O	N
11	20	13	10	22		1	13	8	14	13	3	12	6	3

48.

M	A	Y	A		A	N	G	E	L	O	U
20	2	22	2		2	3	16	11	10	6	19

49.

A	L	I	C	E		W	A	L	K	E	R
2	10	13	8	11		7	2	10	14	11	5

50.

R	O	B	E	R	T		L	U	D	L	U	M
5	6	4	11	5	18		10	19	1	10	19	20